Y0-DJM-846

395
ZEL

C.2 Zeldis, Yona   52559
Coping with social
situations

95-19265

Title II - ESEA 92-93

HR

DATE DUE	BORROWER'S NAME	
MY 11 '98	Ashley L Hall	310
3/11/03	Theresa Yohnes	402
1/30/14	Angelica Guzman	
	Hey Morales	1

395
ZEL

95-19265

ZELDIS, YONA   Title II — ESEA
COPING WITH
SOCIAL SITUATIONS   52559

Lourdes High School Library
4034 West 56th Street
Chicago, Illinois 60629

Coping With Social Situations
A Handbook of Correct Behavior

by
Yona Zeldis

The Rosen Publishing Group
New York

Lourdes High School Library
4034 West 56th Street
Chicago, Illinois 60629

Published in 1984, 1987 by The Rosen Publishing Group, Inc.
29 East 21st Street, New York, NY 10010

Revised Edition 1987
Copyright 1984, 1987 by Yona Zeldis

All rights reserved. No part of this book may be
reproduced in any form without permission in writing
from the publisher, except by a reviewer.

52559

Library of Congress Cataloging in Publication Data

Zeldis, Yona.
    Coping with social situations.
    Includes index

    1. Etiquette for children and youth.   I. Title.
BJ1857.C5Z44   1984   395'.123   84-11661
ISBN 0-8239-0767-8

95-19265

Manufactured in the United States of America

395
ZEL
c. 2

About the author

Although born in Israel, Yona Zeldis was brought up in the borough of Brooklyn and considers herself to be a native New Yorker. She received an A.B. in Art History in 1979 from Vassar College which was soon followed by an M.A. from Columbia University.

Ms. Zeldis has a broad range of literary interests: she has written fiction and criticism, in addition to public relations material and speeches.

She currently lives and works in New York and is actively pursuing her career as a free-lance writer.

Contents

Preface

All of us have complex, multifaceted natures. Our person-
alities and characters have many aspects. Different situations
call forth different emotions in us, caus`ng us to respond and
react in a variety of ways. There is the person we are with our
family, the people to whom we are most intimately connected.
There is the person we are when alone, with only our own
thoughts to absorb us. And there is the person we are in public,
at school, at work, with friends and acquaintances. That you
might say is our social self, and it is to that aspect of our nature
that this book is addressed. We all want to be at our best socially
and to make a good impression on others, but sometimes it is
difficult, confusing. I hope that this book will answer some questions and resolve some doubts, and that through it you can
achieve the poise, ease, and confidence that make socializing so
pleasurable.

CHAPTER I

It All Begins at Home: Getting Along with Your Family

"What does being socially adept have to do with my family?" you may wonder. "After all, I certainly don't have to impress them!" While it may be true that family members know you better than outsiders and are closer to you, there still are certain codes of social behavior that apply even within that intimate circle. Being close to people doesn't mean that you can feel free to abuse or mistreat them or walk all over their feelings. Your family deserves the same respect and consideration you show to outsiders. And since being socially graceful and poised is something that is learned, and not innate, why not start right here, in your very own home?

For many teenagers, home life can be filled with all sorts of minor irritations. Your parents nag you, disapprove of your friends, pester you to help more with household chores. Your kid sister swipes your lipsticks and uses them to draw pictures, or hides your diary and threatens to read it to your friends. Your parents won't let you use the car, and complain about the phone bills. At times you wish you could run off to some remote tropical island and never have to deal with any of them again . . .

This chapter cannot offer any secrets for an ever-smooth and harmonious family existence, but you can use it to explore some major areas of tension at home and to help formulate your own ideas about how to alleviate them.

Do Unto Others . . .

The Golden Rule should have special application for those with whom you must live. The very first thing to remember is that you should show family members the same respect and consideration that you would want directed toward yourself. That can mean anything from speaking gently and politely to a younger sibling (even if you sometimes think that he or she is a little brat!) to doing favors when asked and generally being respectful of others' rights and feelings. Don't snoop through other people's belongings. Don't borrow possessions without permission. Don't wake people up if it's not necessary. Pick up your own clutter; don't wait for someone else to do it. Do things without being told. Don't indulge in cruel teasing. Treat the belongings of your family members with care, not disdain or indifference.

Your Parents

As long as you live with your parents and they are responsible for the food on the table and the roof over your head, you owe them a certain amount of respect and consideration. When you are living on your own and supporting yourself, you can come home at any hour of the day or night, talk on the phone nonstop for hours, leave your socks, baseball jacket, magazines, and records strewn about with abandon—but not while you're still living with your folks.

If your mother expects you home for dinner, it is your responsibility to be there on time. If you find that you can't make it, show her the courtesy of a phone call in advance to explain your absence and tell her what time you can be expected. Don't expect to be waited on hand and foot when you get in either; you are old enough to get your own dinner and clean up after yourself.

Obeying the Rules

That can mean curfews and rules about dating, schoolwork, and household tasks. It is natural (and often expected) for teens to be somewhat rebellious and to assert their independence from their parents. But you must consider that independence is earned. As long as your parents are taking care of you, you must obey them and abide by their wishes in the home. The more you are able to accept maturely the limitations they place on you, the more open and receptive they will be to your desire for increased independence and privileges.

Address Your Parents with Respect

When one of your parents asks you a question, you should respond by saying "Yes, Father" or "No, Mother" rather than mumbling "Yeah" or "Nah." Don't ignore your parents' queries and demands, even if you feel that they are being too inquisitive. Better to say, "I would rather not discuss that" in a reasonable and polite tone of voice than to pretend you didn't hear or storm out of the room slamming the door behind you.

Housework

It *is* a drag, and no one really wants to do it. But unless we have a full-time maid, cook, butler, and secretary, housework is something that all of us have to live with. Perhaps one of the main causes of tension on the subject is a misunderstanding about the daily requirements in a family and who is going to meet them. If you feel that this is true in your family, perhaps you can be the one to suggest gathering everyone together for a family meeting. Make a chart if you like, listing all the chores such as dishes, sweeping and vacuuming, dusting, and walking the dog. Be sure to leave spaces for how often the job needs doing and who is going to be responsible for it. Some families prefer to assign a particular task to one person: Johnny may like raking leaves whereas his brother Tom prefers taking care of the three cats. Or you may want to rotate chores: Each person is assigned to set the table one night of the week, clear it another, and wash the dishes on a third. Whichever way your family selects, it is a good idea to meet and discuss it openly so that you are all clear about your roles and obligations within the family structure.

Parents Are Only Human

As children, we see our parents as infinitely older, wiser, more powerful, and experienced than we are. But as we grow into maturity and adulthood some of those perceptions begin to diminish and fade. You come to realize that your parents are just people, with all the strengths and weaknesses, virtues and failings to which all people are subject. Your father and mother work hard, no doubt, either in the home or outside of it. They have financial worries, worries about their children, and possibly worries about their own parents and their inevitable old age.

As a young person with your whole life ahead of you, you should remember those things when judging your parents' behavior. If they occasionally seem preoccupied or irritable, try to understand the source of such feelings. When they turn to you for a favor or help or support, cooperate with them. You are no longer a child, and an open, happy relationship at home is partly your responsibility. You have to show your parents that you deserve the freedom and privileges you want. Remembering a few basic points will help you in your dealings with your parents.

Be polite to your parents' friends. Address them by name and make it a point to chat with them when they stop by the house or call on the telephone. They are guests in your home, and you should show them the proper courtesy. And you do want to make a good impression and to give your parents reason to be proud of you.

Be respectful. That may mean holding doors or offering a seat. Showing your parents a little deference around the house will certainly improve their response to your requests and demands.

Talk to your parents. That may sound odd, considering that you do live with these people, but think about it for a moment. When was the last time you had a serious conversation with either of your parents about religion, politics, a book or movie, their childhood, or any other subject that is important to either of you? Sometimes it is all too easy to take them for granted: You may spend much of your time at home in your room with the headphones on, talking to a friend on the telephone, or stretched out in front of the television set.

Try to probe your parents just a little and get them to share their feelings on important thoughts and issues. Ask them about their own teenage years. Were their concerns the same as yours? Different? And why? Sound them out about their beliefs and opinions; they may surprise you with their knowledge. Let your parents know a little about you, too. Many teens feel the need for privacy and in some cases even secrecy, but parents often understand a lot more than you might expect. Try sharing some of your future plans and aspirations with them. Take the time to tell them about what you're doing in school, your friends, your social life. They may not agree with you, or always approve, but you will have laid the groundwork for a rich and rewarding relationship with the people who brought you into the world— and, after all, isn't that what family life is all about?

Siblings

Unless you are an only child, you have to deal with brothers or sisters or any combination thereof. They can seem like terrible nuisances at times, but if you learn to show one another a little respect and courtesy, you may find that they can also be the very best of friends.

When you have younger brothers or sisters, you may be asked to baby-sit for them from time to time. If you are not too resentful of the demand, you can make it into a pleasure rather than a burden. Respecting children's dignity sets the proper example and teaches them the way to become courteous and dignified.

Remember, these traits are learned best by example, not words. If you rudely yank something out of your little sister's hand while telling her that she must learn to be polite, you are only confusing her and wasting your breath. Treat her as a friend, and she may soon learn to behave like one. Ask your little sister or brother questions and listen to the answers. Don't exclude a younger sibling from all of your activities. That will give you better justification for the times when you do want to be alone, and your wishes are more likely to be accepted without a fuss than if you are constantly rejecting and pushing away. If, for instance, you invite your little sister to the movies with your friends one afternoon, she will probably understand it better when you tell her the next night that you would prefer to spend time with them alone. Learning to compromise brings better results for all concerned.

If your siblings are older than you, you may be in a different position. Try to be sensitive to others' right to be alone, and they will be more apt to include you in activities than if you are constantly being a pest. Don't borrow or use things belonging to a sibling without asking, especially things that you know are important to the other person, such as favorite articles of clothing, sports equipment, a camera, or a stereo set. Again, you will find that siblings are more generous with their belongings if you show the proper respect.

Privacy

Let's face it, by their very nature, family life and privacy contradict each other. Family life is simply not solitary; it is cooperative and communal. It involves sharing and compromises, negotiations and adjustments. That is precisely why privacy—your own and that of other family members with whom you must live—is so critical. In order not to feel invaded, or to invade others, we all need to set clear limits and boundaries on the time and space that we call our own.

Sharing a Room

You may be lucky and live in a rambling, spacious house with a room all to yourself. Whenever you are feeling moody, sad, introspective, or just plain unsociable, you can close the door and retreat from the world for a while. But many, if not most, teens have to share a room with one or even two siblings and so need a different way of defining their own space at home.

If possible, establish something that is solely and exclusively your own in the room. It may be a dresser, a desk, a shelf in the closet, a favorite chair, your own bed—whatever. It will be a place that you have the rights to and you alone can decide whether or not to share it. Remember that staking out your own territory means giving others the same courtesy and living up to your end of the bargain; don't start encroaching upon the space of others without an express invitation.

Once that has been established, you can afford to be magnanimous and share some things with your siblings. You will find that it is easier to share when you know there is something that is specially and uniquely your own. And you will find that to be true of your siblings: the more you respect their privacy, the more generous they are likely to be.

Emotional Privacy

Physical space is one thing; emotional space is perhaps even more important between family members. That means learning to ask without prying into the affairs of others, and also knowing when to stop asking. It means *never* giving in to the temptation of eavesdropping; reading letters, diaries, or journals that belong to another person; listening in on phone conversations, or going through someone else's possessions. You want to establish an atmosphere of trust and respect in your home, both with siblings and with parents, and so you must do your best to set a good example and to treat others the way you want to be treated yourself.

Telephone Tactics

One of the biggest causes of arguments at home is the use (or misuse!) of the telephone. Following are some basic ways of avoiding conflicts and tension in your household.

1. *Limit your calls.* When your family includes four people or more, it is both considerate and courteous to place a time limit— say fifteen to twenty minutes—on your phone calls. If there is a need to exceed that, try checking with parents and siblings *first*—and avoid lengthy arguments later.

2. *Take messages.* If people call your parents or siblings while they are out, be sure to write down the name of the caller, the date and time of the call, and a return telephone number if it is given to you. The courtesy will be appreciated, and chances are that it will be reciprocated.

3. *Be flexible.* If you have been chatting on the phone for five minutes and suddenly notice your sister gesturing frantically for you to get off, oblige her and do it—as long as she doesn't make a habit of it! Emergencies do arise, and sometimes another household member must break into your call. If you are gracious about it, you will find that the same privilege is extended to you when you need it.

4. *Keep reasonable telephone hours.* Discourage friends from calling late at night, early in the morning, during meals, or at any other time when they might disturb your family's routines.

5. *Limit your long-distance calls.* Nothing adds dollars to the telephone bill each month like long toll calls. Use discretion and make yours brief. Also try to call long distance at times when rates are lower, such as evenings and weekends.

Finally, if all else fails, you might consider getting (and paying for!) your very own phone, with a private number. Or perhaps you can agree to share the cost—and use—with a sibling. That alleviates friction in many homes, but remember that you are responsible for the major portion—if not all—of the expense.

The Bathroom

The use of the bathroom is another major source of household headaches. Mom wants to take a shower, your sister has to set her hair, you've got a big date tonight, and your brother wants to soak the knee he hurt in football practice. Unfortunately, installing a new bathroom is a lot more costly and difficult than installing a new phone. But here are some basic hints that will help keep everyone from flying off the handle.

Schedule. In the mornings, when everyone is rushing to get to work or school, try to adhere to a schedule and take your five, ten, or fifteen minutes at a regular time, so that others don't stand around fuming. Or consider changing routines: Switch your morning shower to an evening one and have plenty of time to enjoy the suds and steam with no one pounding on the door. If you're planning a scented bubble bath, manicure, pedicure, and shampoo, alert other family members beforehand so that they can get in and out before you and thus avoid friction.

Keep it clean. It is your responsibility to clean up after yourself in the bathroom. Don't leave wet towels strewn all over the floor or dusting powder coating every surface. Other people use this room too.

If your house is short of bathrooms, what about additional mirrors (with proper lighting) placed in strategic locations. Then when Dad wants his shave and you want to pile on the paint, there won't be any conflict.

The Family Car

Most teenagers are eager to use the family car as much and as often as they can. But if you want to be trusted in a situation that demands maturity, judgment, and responsibility, you have to convince your parents by the example you set, not simply by the eloquence of your arguments. When you are permitted to take the family car for an outing, remember:

- Never let a friend drive the car unless your parents know about it and have given their complete approval.
- Never drive without your license.
- Don't overload the car; agreeing to give eight people a lift to the party is not wise.
- Fasten your seatbelt, and insist that other passengers fasten theirs.
- If you are driving a long distance, don't make it a marathon. Stop occasionally for a breath of fresh air, to stretch your legs, or have a cup of coffee.
- Don't be reckless. No playing chicken on the road, speeding, making U-turns, sharp corners, sudden stops, just to impress the guys. Your life and theirs are at stake. If you're looking for thrills, get them on a roller coaster, not on the highway.
- Never drive when you've had anything to drink. Ask someone else to drive, or call your parents.

Stepparents and Stepsiblings

After a divorce or a death in the family, your mother or father may remarry. That can be an awkward situation at first. How do you handle this stranger in your midst, or possibly strangers if you also have a new brother or sister?

Remembering that it is a difficult time for everyone is a good place to start. You may feel uncomfortable with the new person in your family circle, but try to imagine the situation from his or her point of view. He or she is probably as uncomfortable as you are and as anxious to be liked and to make a good impression. Your mother or father is no doubt experiencing anxiety too, wondering how the transition will be made and whether everyone will get along.

Make an effort to get to know your new family. Spend some time alone with a new stepparent, or invite a stepsibling to go with you on a walk, to the movies, or on another outing. You may never become the closest of friends, but you might as well make life at home as pleasant as possible for all concerned.

In this situation, it is even more important to be clear about responsibilities and privacy. Make sure that you express your feelings, in a polite and respectful manner, rather than keeping them pent up inside you. Let your new family know about your particular likes and pet peeves, and give them the opportunity to share the same information with you.

If at all possible, don't turn to Mom or Dad to settle every dispute or argument. Try to resolve issues in a grownup way, directly with the person involved. There may be problems of a more serious nature; if so, try turning to a family friend or to a guidance counselor or teacher to whom you feel close.

Get to know your new family in your own way, at your own pace. Closeness and intimacy take time to develop. If the new family members seem strange for a while, keep extending yourself and don't give up because the situation doesn't change all at once.

Living With an Older Family Member

At some point you may live with one or both of your grandparents, or perhaps an elderly aunt or uncle. As a responsible and mature person, you must treat this person with all the warmth and respect that you would give any other family member.

Older people are sometimes less receptive to changes in their routines or habits. You may not like it, or agree, but you should still defer to the wishes of an older person living in your household, particularly insofar as the issue affects them directly. Your grandmother may have very particular notions about the way her food is served or the arrangement of her room; that is her right, and you should respect her feelings.

Age can become debilitating, and your grandmother or grandfather may develop physical infirmities with which you must learn to cope. Keep in mind that we all grow old, and that caring for the elderly is an important and often meaningful responsibility. If you understand that, you will begin to learn compassion and patience from the experience. You can accommodate weaknesses without pity or scorn by imagining yourself in a similar situation. Speak slowly and clearly to a person who has trouble hearing; offer to read to a person whose eyesight is failing; lend a shoulder or an arm to a person who finds walking difficult. Many young people find themselves deeply enriched by the privilege of having lived with and helped care for an older family member.

CHAPTER II

Moving Outward: Your Friends

To the young person, the friendships that are established during the teen years seem of critical and vital importance, and in fact that is not untrue. As you begin to move outside your immediate family circle and to think about leaving the secure nest of home, the need to establish other meaningful relationships does become very important. Girls and boys look to their friends for support, empathy, and reassurance about who they are during this time of growth and change. When things go wrong with a friend, a young person is apt to be as heartbroken and unhappy as if the loss were a romantic one. And the lack of friends—the loneliness, isolation, and frustration that are felt—can be among the most painful feelings of adolescence.

How Do I Make Friends?

This is a common query, and so often repeated that it must be addressed at the outset. The answer begins with: "First, you have to meet them." For most teenagers, school provides the ready-made environment in which to meet and get to know people, and the shared activities do provide a basis for many friendships. But sometimes there are obstacles. Someone may live too far from other members of the class to be easily included in group activities. Or a girl may have moved with her family to a new town during her last year in high school, only to find that her classmates are very cliquish and not interested in getting to know anyone outside their chosen circle.

"Those first three months were horrible for me," confesses Jenny, a slender brunette with bright dark eyes. "All the girls in my class would whisper and giggle when I came into the room. It felt like a conspiracy or something."

But Jenny didn't give up when she found that her schoolmates were something less than friendly. She had always loved roller-skating, and she looked through the yellow pages to find a nearby rink where she could indulge in her favorite pastime. She became a regular there, and within a matter of weeks found not one but two girls who admired her ability on skates. It turned out that one of them attended her school and could give her the necessary introductions to the "in" group. Nowadays, Jenny has as active a social life as anyone could want. "Sometimes," she confides with a smile, "I don't even get to skate as much as I would like!"

The lesson is clear: An activity for which you have a real affinity is likely to yield new friends. Enthusiasm is always contagious, and people respond to it. If you like tennis, get out there on the courts and play. If it's swimming that you love, find the local pool. Nor need you confine yourself to what you do well. If you've always wanted to try your hand at painting, and it's not offered at your school, sign up for a class somewhere else. Maybe you've always had a yen to be on the stage; is there a drama group or club that you could join? Few things create the kind of bond that comes from working together over sets and rehearsals. Let your interests and desires lead the way; the rest will happen almost of its own accord.

Getting to Know You

Say you have no trouble making friends—only keeping them. Some trouble always seems to surface, and there you are, facing a big rift with a close friend and feeling just terrible. Keeping a friendship thriving and growing is a wonderful thing, but it takes work. Honesty, respect, commitment, empathy—those qualities are to friendship as sunlight, good soil, and fresh water are to plants. "Well, that's easy enough," you think, "I can offer all that." But can you? Sometimes, it's not as easy as it seems. Let's say a friend asks you to read a paper that he's just finished for your history class. He's worked hard on it and now wants the benefit of another opinion. You read it, and to your dismay you think it's poorly researched and badly written. How do you tell him without hurting his feelings and discouraging him totally? Or do you lie and tell him you think it's great, even though it deserves a grudging D in your estimation?

A sensitive and thoughtful friend would be truthful without being cruel and would offer positive suggestions instead of just damning criticism. You might start by praising some aspect you thought was good: "I really liked the section..." and then add, "but it would be even stronger if you..." In that way, you can be true to your own feelings while still maintaining a sensitivity to your friend's feelings. You might also consider the nature of the relationship: A close friend of three years' standing is less likely to be wounded by your remarks than someone who is relatively new to your social scheme.

The pleasure of friendship makes it seem as if it just happens, without effort. But like anything of value that we love, it has to be maintained or it runs the risk of dying. When making new friends or planning get-togethers with old ones, keep their likes and dislikes in mind. Don't suggest a hockey game to a quiet, bookish type who knows nothing about sports, or shopping to a tomboy who lives in jeans and her brother's sweatshirts. Try to think of situations in which you can both participate and share the fun.

Friends should not be taken for granted. Birthdays are special events, so treat them as such. Recognize any new achievements or accomplishments: getting into college, winning a contest, getting the lead role in the school play. Friends should support and endorse each other's efforts toward growth.

Just Goofing Around

Even in the most casual settings and situations with your friends, there are still some basic rules of conduct to which you should adhere. Good manners aren't only for grownups and people you don't know; they should be part of the way you interact with everyone.

Don't interrupt when someone else is speaking. Let the other person finish a thought before you have your say. Don't be a conversation hog either. When you have been talking for a long time, stop and let someone else have the floor.

Don't be chronically late. Accidents and emergencies happen; anyone can forgive a car that broke down, or a train that stalled. But don't keep your friends waiting for you every time. Be prompt and keep your word. Someone who makes everyone else miss the first ten minutes of the movie or stand around in the cold isn't going to be considered very good company.

Do be generous. If you can easily baby-sit for a friend's little sister, do it. Offer a lift, or to help out with the party decorations. That doesn't mean being a doormat and letting others take unfair advantage of you. But remember, generosity and consideration for others go a long way in making and keeping friends.

Don't be overly critical. As mentioned earlier, honesty is important, but it should never be used as a weapon. Be sure you couch criticism in the gentlest, kindest, and most constructive terms.

Be careful about gossip. It would be unrealistic to admonish you never to talk about other people. But do remember that repeating unkind gossip makes your listeners wonder what you say about them behind their backs. Never repeat something that a friend has told you in confidence; there is no surer way to violate the trust that he or she has placed in you.

Don't make a friend a psychiatrist. Sharing problems and concerns is one thing; constantly seeking advice and support is another. Be intimate, but don't abuse the privilege. If your problems are getting out of hand, see someone who is qualified to help you cope. You will be doing a favor to your friend—and to yourself.

Don't feel that all your friends must get along. Katie is a fun-loving extrovert who loves punk rock music and dancing until dawn; Jill is quiet and introspective and never without a good book in hand. Is it necessary to bring them together? Savor the qualities you enjoy in each separately and make sure to spend time with each alone or in groups that might mix more comfortably. Not all your friends will get along equally well together, nor need they.

These basic rules grow out of the simple respect that is the basis of any good and enduring friendship.

The Inner Circle

Although we hate to admit it, our time and resources are limited, and we cannot offer the same amount of time to everyone, even all of our friends. There may be one friend whose companionship we value above all others.

"Jack has been like a brother to me," says Bill, an athletic high school senior. "I made new friends when I went to college, but no one has ever been able to take his place."

This kind of feeling for another person is quite special, and you cannot hope to duplicate it in every friendship you make. We all create private hierarchies, which are perfectly fine as long as we are sensitive and careful about revealing them to others.

Say you have one friend with whom you like to play chess. You may not see much of this person aside from an occasional game, but you do enjoy his or her company and the stimulation of your game. Perhaps it is not a person you would confide in or with whom you would share your inner thoughts, but that doesn't lessen the value of what you do have together. The fact that not all friendships are equal in their intensity doesn't detract from their merit or worth.

FRIENDS AND FAMILY

Naturally, you want your family to approve of the friendships you make, and you hope that your friends can feel comfortable in your home, interacting with your family members. In order to insure that this union be a happy and congenial one for all concerned, you might want to consider some basic rules:

Always ask. Perhaps you want your best friend to stay to supper or spend the weekend. Or you may be thinking of throwing an impromptu party and asking a few friends over to listen to records. Make sure that you consult with your parents and that it is a comfortable time to have guests. Maybe your mother isn't feeling well, or your father has brought home a lot of work, and tonight isn't the best for a social gathering. Your parents will be a lot more receptive to your friends if you keep their needs in mind before doing any inviting.

Abide by the rules. If your parents set a midnight curfew but you and the guys always seem to come in about 1:00 a.m., don't expect a warm reception for Bill, Tom, Karl, and Hank when they next come to pick you up. You know they are a great bunch, but you may find yourself grounded and your friends banned for a while. Parents tend to believe that other people are leading their own teens astray; hence the prohibitions. It's much easier if you can accept the limitations your parents impose; they in turn will respect your efforts and may allow you more freedom in recognition of your maturity. Their attitude toward your crowd will probably improve, too.

Treat your home with respect. When you are having people over, be sure that your friends' high spirits don't cause them to break Mom's favorite oriental vase or stain the brand-new carpeting. Don't abuse your home. If damage does occur, offer to pay for it and keep your promise. That rule works well in reverse: If you want to be a welcome guest, treat the homes of your friends with respect, too.

When in Rome

While we're on the subject of other people's homes, it is worth addressing a few words to proper conduct when at the homes of your friends and classmates. Remember that a good guest is someone who is always invited back and whose visit is looked forward to with pleasure; a poor or rude guest is someone whose leaving is looked upon with relief.

Many of the rules we have been discussing apply here as well. Be a lively conversationalist, but don't insist on all the attention for yourself. Try to draw others out, and engage them in a conversation, not a monologue.

Treat the possessions of others with care and respect. No feet on the sofa or the cocktail table. If you smoke, use the ashtray, and if you don't see one, ask!

Give your hosts the courtesy of expecting your visit. Don't drop in unless you are sure that if your visit is ill-timed your host can easily say so without embarrassing you or himself. When you're "just in the neighborhood," a quick phone call takes very little time and can go a long way toward putting everyone at ease.

Try to conform to the general preferences of your hosts or the other guests. If the main course is salmon and you dislike fish, you might be polite and eat it anyway. However, if there are reasons of health or religion for not eating something that is served, you may want to inform your hostess.

"I just wanted to let you know, Mrs. Inness, that I'm a vegetarian" will do more to win her good graces than if you simply refuse to touch her standing rib roast with no word of explanation.

On the subject of gifts, use discretion. Hostess gifts may be an old-fashioned custom, but it is nonetheless charming and endearing, perhaps all the more so for having fallen into disuse. If invited for a meal, do take something. It needn't be much: a small bunch of flowers (yes, you can pick them yourself!), candy, wine, some baked treat (again, if you bake it yourself, all the better!) are all good bets. The same goes for weekend visits. If you want your friend's parents to invite you back to their lovely lakeside country house, you might make yourself stand out in their minds by the thoughtful gesture of a small gift. For lengthier stays, a thank-you note is always appreciated.

Don't expect to be waited on hand and foot, either. A good

guest will offer to clear the table and dry the dishes. Your hosts may refuse, which is their prerogative, but you should still make the offer—especially when you are staying for the night. An overnight guest should make the bed in the morning, fold the towels, and not strew belongings all over the living room. No matter how much at home your hosts make you feel, you shouldn't abuse their hospitality.

Other Tips for Weekends Away

Try to adapt your own habits to those of your hosts. If they are a family of early risers, don't sleep until eleven, even though you might do so at home. You needn't be up at the crack of dawn with them, but compromise and tailor your behavior accordingly. If, on the other hand, they get up late and you like to see the sun rise, by all means do so, but be quiet and allow them to sleep undisturbed. You may be accustomed to practicing the French horn first thing in the morning, but you would be well advised to drop the notion for the duration of your visit and read the morning paper or a book instead.

Dress appropriately. Make sure you know in advance what weekend activities are in store. If horseback riding is on the agenda, don't get stuck with three party dresses and two pairs of heels. But if all you pack are jeans and T-shirts and church is the Sunday morning ritual, you are bound to feel out of place. The same applies for the weather: Although your host or hostess would be more than happy to lend a sweater or a sunhat, you will be more comfortable if you go prepared. Another tip: Do pack a bathrobe. You may feel perfectly at ease waltzing around in your baby-doll nightie or your torn old pajamas, but don't assume that your hosts will feel equally comfortable. Wear a wrapper or robe to and from the bathroom at night and in the morning. And dress for breakfast, unless you are told otherwise.

WE'RE HAVING A PARTY

Most people love parties, looking forward to being invited to a gala event and to throwing one of their own. Party-going and party-giving require some thought and preparation. You'll find that as you get more experienced with the process you'll enjoy yourself more and worry less. The discomfort some people feel at such events can be easily alleviated if you take the time to think and plan ahead.

When You're the Guest

First find out what kind of party it is going to be. A huge bash with dozens of people from many different places? A smaller dinner party with a few close friends? A surprise birthday party? Be sure you know in advance so that you can derive the greatest pleasure from it. Part of growing up involves realizing that you are responsible (in part, of course) for your own pleasure and enjoyment; what you give to something has a direct relationship to what you gain from it.

When you know what kind of party you are attending, find out if anyone you know is going. Arrange for a way to get there and home again. That is especially important at nighttime events; parents tend to worry, so ease their minds and make some plans. Think about what you want to wear. Is it a casual affair, with everyone in jeans, or will it require more formal attire? If the latter, plan in advance. Have your best suit cleaned and your tie pressed. Don't show up with safety pins tacking up your hem or a in a dress borrowed from your sister, two sizes too big and a dreadful color besides. You will feel more confident and relaxed if you are dressed appropriately.

What Can You Do?

This question is really for you to interpret. Do you want to offer a ride, or your flair for decorating? Can you bake a terrific devil's food cake, or bring the popcorn and pretzels? Is there punch that needs mixing or a den that can use some tidying? Participation is the key to respect, and respect often brings more invitations your way. People will feel that you are reliable, dependable, and generally the sort of person they want to have around. Do take a gift to a party. If it's a birthday, graduation party, shower, or the like, the present can be personal and reflect something unique about the recipient. If it's a larger, less specific occasion, make the gift more general. Seasonal gifts are fun, too. At Halloween you might make a pumpkin pie or carve your very own jack-o'-lantern; Christmas might inspire you to take a wonderfully scented wreath or glittering ornaments for the tree.

On the Scene

People sometimes do worry about parties. What can I say, they wonder, how can I meet people? That is natural and happens to everyone from time to time, even the most seasoned partygoer. Don't feel too isolated. Being prepared always helps, of course, and if you've done your homework you'll have a good head start. But suppose you're at a fairly large party, where you know only a few people. You're dressed casually, like everyone else in the crowd, but your jeans have been freshly laundered and pressed and your sweater is new and one of your favorites. You've brought a small gift with you, and you've said hello to Maggie, the hostess. Now what? The few people you know seem to have disappeared, and you're starting to feel a little awkward. Your palms are .wet, and your mouth is going dry and . . .

First: Don't panic. Other people sometimes feel that way, too. Remember, you're here to have a good time—now, what are you going to do about it?

Talk. Don't be afraid to strike up a conversation with people standing next to you, even if you've never laid eyes on them before. Most people are flattered by it and are relieved and eager to talk to you. And don't worry about "clever" opening lines: The point is to be warm and friendly. You might start off by saying, "I know Maggie from my French class—what about you?" That gives you a common point of reference—your hostess. Even if the other person doesn't know her, chances are he or she was brought by someone who does, and once the story begins to unfold, voila! there's your conversation, happening all by itself.

Don't be afraid to compliment people. Try to say things that you mean, but it never hurts to be kind. Start by observing, "That's a lovely dress you have on; the color really suits you. Where did you get it?" and watch the ball begin rolling. It's hard for anyone to resist a little harmless flattery, and you should feel free to indulge in it. Don't go overboard, though; insincerity and lying are obvious to most people, and they will quickly become mistrustful.

Other openers can be equally simple and straightforward: "I live in _____; do you live nearby?" or "Do you go to _____ School, too?" or even "I'm _____. What's your name?" Again, don't agonize over trying to sound witty or sophisticated. Most people will respond with pleasure and enthusiasm to a friendly overture and be only too happy to converse with you. If, for some unknown reason, you are rebuffed, try not to take it personally and move on. The person may be involved in things that have nothing to do with you. As an adult, you must learn to recognize that not every rejection is a judgment about you.

Keep in mind that if you're feeling shy you can always turn to your host or hostess and ask him or her to make some introductions for you. Just say, "Excuse me, Bob, but I don't seem to know many of your friends. Do you think you could make a couple of introductions?" and you'll be on your way.

Party smarts. Remember the rules for other social situations that have been outlined, and you'll be fine. Don't be the last to leave. Get a sense of the evening's flow. When the party begins to thin out, make a graceful exit. Be sure to say good-night to your host and give your thanks for the invitation. Say good-night to your friends too, and if you've made a new friend try to strengthen the bond a little by suggesting a future get-together or phone call.

When You're the Host or Hostess

Planning a bash takes a little more preparation than attending one, but with practice it can be easily and successfully accomplished. The ability to throw terrific parties, where the guests always have a wonderful time and are sorry to leave, is one of the nicest skills you can acquire as you move into adulthood.

Decisions, Decisions

As a guest you had to do a bit of thinking about where, when, and why, but now you must do a good deal more. First, you may want to consult your parents, since it is probably their home you will be using. Get a sense of their limitations and restrictions: Your small house may not hold fifty of your classmates, and a more select guest list would be in order. Once you've decided what kind of party you're throwing—buffet brunch or afternoon barbecue—start making lists. Decide on the guests and what you need in the way of preparation and food, and make a rough timetable for what needs to be done beforehand. You'll probably need some help. Maybe you can enlist the aid of some close friends or family members, but be careful not to abdicate responsibility. Don't say that you want to host a party and then expect Mom and your kid sister to do all the work. You have to be prepared to take charge and to organize. A good captain must be fully in control before he or she can start parceling out chores and assigning responsibilities.

Food

Think about the kinds of refreshments you want to serve: Will you have a sit-down meal at Mom's big mahogany table, complete with candles and place cards? Do you want a buffet lunch alfresco? Or will you just serve snacks such as cheese, fruit, crackers, and dips?

Money will of course be a concern. Create a budget early, and stick to it. Caviar and duckling are certainly elegant party fare—but not for sixty guests. You might want to think about chili and chips for a crowd that size. Keep your limitations clearly in mind, and you won't be tempted to go overboard.

If your budget is really tight and you still want to entertain, you could have a potluck party to which each guest brings some treat. Casseroles, fruit salads, coleslaw, cookies, brownies, and cheese and crackers all make easily transportable and inexpensive party eating.

Decorations

A party is a special event, outside of the ordinary daily routine. Its setting, then, should reflect that. Start with a good housecleaning. Shine windows, clean floors, throw open doors and windows for a fresh, airy breeze. A well-scrubbed room is the right basis for any form of adornment. And think how pleased Mom will be!

The decorations you choose can be simple. Keep the season in mind. Fresh flowers from your yard in the spring, ears of richly colored Indian corn in the fall make attractive party centerpieces. Don't overlook the traditional balloons and crepe paper streamers; they are inexpensive and make for a festive mood.

Guests

Sending invitations may be out of date, but it is a custom you should think about reviving. Whether your party is large or small, formal or casual, it's always nice to send something to announce the event. Buy printed invitations in a card shop, or be creative and make your own, using colored paper and Magic Markers. Or you can just write a simple announcement in a nice script (see if you can achieve some skill with an italic nib) and have it photocopied. However you do it, people will automatically sit up and take notice—you've gone to some trouble, and now they probably will too.

Think carefully about your guest list. It's fine to invite people who don't know each other, but be sure to provide introductions for your guests when they arrive. Also, unless you are opting for a single-sex party such as a sleep-over with all the girls in the class, try to keep the number of males and females fairly even. This rule is not rigid; don't worry about an extra girl or two, but any gathering of ten males and two females is bound to be a little lopsided.

Dress

In the invitation, you can let your guests know what to wear. If some are dressed in jeans and others in three-piece suits, someone is bound to feel out of place. As the host or hostess, you should be attractively dressed. It may be the most casual of get-togethers, but showing up in dirty jeans and a torn sweatshirt is insulting to your guests and denies the very sense of occasion that you are trying to create. A better choice might be a pair of casual but neat pants, teamed with an attractive sweater for a boy and a pretty blouse and beads for a girl.

The Big Night

You've done all your planning and preparation: scrubbed the house and yourself, prepared the food. The guests have arrived, there's music on, and the party is in full swing. Now what? Can you just relax and enjoy yourself? If everything seems to be running smoothly, the answer is yes. You should have a good time at your own party; after all, that's why you threw it in the first place. But a good host or hostess will remain alert and ward off any potential difficulties.

That can mean anything from making sure that the punch bowl is full and the serving dishes are replenished to dealing with an obstreperous guest. In the latter case, don't hesitate to call on Mom or Dad for assistance. There's a good reason for parties to be chaperoned, and this is one of them. You can't assume all the responsibility yourself; sometimes you need the intervention of an adult.

The object is to keep things flowing. Distribute the refreshments throughout the room to keep people from getting jammed up in one area. If you see someone looking lost and lonely, introduce him or her to a group or ask for help with some small task. If you're having music, keep records and tapes handy and vary the selections played.

The Morning After

No one expects you to wash every used dish and glass and pick up every crumpled napkin at 3 a.m., but you should be prepared to assume the lion's share of the clean-up job the next day. It was your party, after all, and it's the surest way to convince your folks that you are grownup enough to assume the responsibilities of a host or hostess. And there will be fewer objections when the next shindig rolls around.

CHAPTER III

Clothes Make the Man (or Woman):
Some Thoughts on Dress

We have all heard that beauty is only skin deep and that appearance is only superficial. Our real worth lies within, we are told, and has little to do with the exterior. That may be partly true, but it is also somewhat naive. Most of us respond immediately to the physical appearance of another person: fear, attraction, longing, dislike, admiration, awe are all emotions that may arise, rightly or wrongly, from knowing nothing about a person but the way he or she looks. And if we are honest, we acknowledge that others respond to us in similar fashion.

There is nothing wrong with those responses; they are woven into our system of values, customs, and beliefs. No, we should not be entirely influenced by someone's looks: The most beautiful girl in the class may be cold and heartless, the handsomest boy, silly and vain. Ultimately, true worth does lie within. But first we need to attract people to us so that they can discover the riches inside. And the surest way to do that is by looking our very best. Clothing is an integral part of looking well, but before we even approach the topic of what we put on our bodies, we need to pay some attention to the bodies themselves.

Most teens are blessed with good metabolism and lead active lives, so that keeping physically fit is relatively easy. No one, least of all you, should demand that your body resemble that of a professional athlete or model. But for your own health and good looks, you should make exercise a regular part of your life. The trick is to find something that you like to do so that you have a built-in incentive to keep at it. If you despise jogging, it will be pretty difficult to adhere to a regimen that demands three miles a day at the crack of dawn. Be realistic. Try swimming or riding a bicycle instead, if those are activities you prefer. The point is enjoyment as well as health.

Don't think exclusively about planned sports or exercise. If you walk ten blocks instead of taking a bus and use the stairs instead of an elevator, you are developing habits that will keep you fit and trim throughout your life.

Finally, concentrate on your own fun and recreation. If you do like to run, see if you can do it around a scenic park or lake to enhance your pleasure. Learn a new sport or try a new activity: ballet classes, aerobics, water skiing, or horseback riding all may be welcome departures from your usual routine. In fact, you may have so much fun that you'll forget you're doing something that's good for you. Taking care of your body should be a pleasure, not a punishment, and good habits developed early will ensure that that remains true.

Heads Up

Everyone looks better when standing straight. Good posture goes hand in hand with exercise, and it is essential for good looks. If yours is less than perfect, practice, practice, practice until you make some improvement. Balance books on your head and walk around your room until you can do it without dropping one. Nothing looks worse than a pretty girl slouching or a handsome boy who can't keep his head up. It's bad for your health, and it makes you look uncomfortable and nervous. So learn to put your best foot forward—by standing tall!

Start with the Basics

Cleanliness is the prerequisite of true beauty. Nothing you wear can make up for a dirty neck, lank hair, and grubby fingernails. Keeping clean outstrips fashion and money, so let a well-scrubbed face and body be the first thing you "put on" every day.

Everyone's personal habits and needs differ, of course, but hygiene starts with plenty of hot water, soap, and shampoo. Girls tend to be more elaborate in their rituals and opt for perfume and cosmetics. Keep in mind, though, that heavy makeup over an unwashed fash will only result in blemishes and break-outs, the bane of every teen-aged girl's existence.

Learn your particular needs as well. Is your skin dry and likely to be flaky or scaly? Then look for a soap with a cream or oil base and follow up with a moisturizer applied to problem spots. If your skin is oily, however, try a long-handled scrub brush or loofah and use astringent to keep blemishes to a minimum.

Your Clothes and You

Your clothing should reflect who you are and be appropriate to what you are doing when you're wearing it. The clothes you wear on weekends with your friends are different from those you wear to school or on big family occasions, so let each outfit express a particular facet or aspect of your personality.

For young people who are in the throes of an identity crisis, clothing may take on extreme symbolic importance and meaning. It helps us define and express ourselves and becomes a quick, almost shorthand way of identifying with our peers. If all the guys at school are wearing leather jackets, snug faded jeans, and cowboy boots, then part of a boy's masculine identity may be bound up in his decision to adopt that mode of dress. A girl makes a specific statement about herself when she opts for pastel colors, ruffles, and lace. To a certain extent, we are what we wear—or at least, we feel that way. Keep in mind what you are trying to project when you select your clothing; you will make your choices more wisely if you think a little of their implications.

Developing a Style

"Style" as defined by Webster's Ninth Collegiate Dictionary is "a distinct manner or custom of behavior or conducting one-self." Teenagers in particular are often obsessed with style—getting it, having it, perfecting it. What they often forget, however, is that "style" used in this way is rarely something that one puts on, like a new dress or pair of jeans, but rather something that is acquired slowly and that needs time, patience, and experience to fully ripen and mature.

Most teens want to be accepted, one of the crowd—in short, they want very much to belong. At the same time, they don't want to look like everyone else. They want to develop a way of being and looking that is distinctly and uniquely their own. Clothing plays an important part in that process. While it may take time to cultivate and refine one's own personal style, the teen years are certainly the time to experiment with it so that it can begin to grow and flower.

The key here is of course *you*. You need to find out who you are, what you like, what you don't like. You need to learn your own strengths and weaknesses and how to use your clothing to enhance your strong points or disguise the weak ones. You want clothing that looks well on *you*, not just in a magazine advertisement. Learning to accept yourself and to evaluate yourself realistically are the first steps in developing a positive sense of your own style. Be critical, but not too harsh. What are your best features? How can you play them up? What do you want to stand out? What would you like to change or conceal?

FOR HIM

Boys usually don't give as much time and thought to their appearance as girls do, but this is a good time for you to start learning some basics. Fashion for men and boys tends to be more conservative and standardized than that designed for women, but don't give up. There are still choices you can make that will accentuate the positive and help you stand out in a crowd.

Consider Your Body Type

Fashion is always changing. What sells like hotcakes one year can't be given away the next. The cut of a jacket may be short or long, the leg on a pair of slacks may taper or widen. But there are some things you can rely on, and one of them is your own physical appearance. Unless you lose or gain large amounts of weight, your teenaged body tends to be the body of your adult life. Get to know it and learn what looks well on you. A longer jacket, padded shoulders, pants with a pleat: You can learn to use these details and others to your advantage in the fashion game. You may have to experiment a bit, but with a little practice you should be able to come up with clothes that make you look your very best.

Think in Color

Color is something that girls tend to be more conscious of, but they certainly shouldn't corner the market on good looks. Are your eyes an attractive shade of green, gray, or blue? Then think about wearing a shirt, tie, or sweater in that shade to pick up and enhance the color. Consider the color of hair and skin too. White shirts against deeply tanned skin are very attractive to the opposite sex; and a dark wool suit on a fair-haired boy can be dramatic and distinctive.

Learn to Accessorize

Good ties, cuff links, a handsome leather belt, your grandfather's antique pocket watch—all these are little extras that can complete and polish your look.

Little Things Count

Wrinkled or soiled clothes can spoil the effect you are trying to create. Boys tend to be more careless about maintenance, so try to grow out of the habit. Jackets peeled off and discarded in

52559

crumpled heaps, shirts that find their way to the bottom of the closet: That's fine for kids who have their moms to pick up after them, but not for young men who have left the world of childhood behind them. Find out what it's like to be responsible for your own laundry and dry cleaning (this goes for girls too!). Take your shoes in for repairs before your mother has to nag you about them. You'll find that these habits pay off in the long run, and your appearance can only improve as a result. No more mismatched socks nor poorly fitting pants, either. The time has come for you to start thinking—and looking—like an adult.

Don't be afraid to seek advice from someone more experienced than yourself. Maybe you want to ask your dad, older brother, or even your girlfriend to accompany you on a shopping trip. You can learn a lot from someone whose taste you respect and admire.

FOR HER

Girls can be romantic, impulsive, and spontaneous. There's nothing wrong with that—except when it's the cause for fashion mistakes.

Remember Who You Are

Don't buy a dress because you saw it on your favorite model or movie actress, especially when she's a five-foot ten-inch blonde and you happen to be a five-foot three-inch brunette. Glamorous advertisements and lavish photo spreads are meant to set you drooling—and spending, so beware. Always keep in mind what works for you and your physical type. With so many alternatives from which to choose, you want to make the best and most flattering decisions possible.

Learn to display your most attractive features and disguise others you find less attractive. If, for example, you've never liked your legs, think about a wardrobe that features several pairs of fashionable pants, and among your footwear you might want to

95-19265

Lourdes High School Library
4034 West 56th Street
Chicago, Illinois 60629

have a couple of pairs of boots. A long graceful throat can be shown off with a scoop-neck sweater or blouse. Narrow skirts can accentute the lines of a svelte figure, while those with fuller proportions can give a sweeping and flattering line to a heavier one.

Fabric pattern has as much effect as the cut of a garment. Bold horizontal stripes will make you look fuller and wider than you are: fine if you're slim and shapely, but definitely something to avoid if you're not. Better to stick with vertical stripes that attenuate the figure or a small overall print on a dark ground. Bold bright colors and white add weight; dark tones and black can create the appearance of slenderness.

Even if you're not concealing anything, you should still keep scale in mind. Exaggerated collars, startling patterns, unexpected pleats, or slits can look well on a girl who is tall and model-like, but a petite figure may be overpowered by such dramatic effects. Conversely, dainty prints, scores of ruffles, and yards of lace may look silly on a tall and big-boned girl.

Acting Your Age

Both boys and girls are apt to want to look older than they are and to strive for the appearance of adulthood. Girls are most likely to try to add years through the use of cosmetics.

Now, makeup for teenaged girls is fine. There is no reason not to take advantage of the rainbow palette offered by the cosmetic companies to enhance your own natural attractiveness. But the key word here is *enhance*—that means highlighting what nature has already given you, not completely reshaping and changing your appearance.

Avoid starkly plucked eyebrows, bizarre eye makeup, and shocking lip colors and blushes. A girl is much more attractive when her own beauty is allowed to shine through. Your daytime makeup might consist of a light foundation, powder, and blush if you feel your skin is less than perfect, but many young girls find that a little pressed powder and blush suits their daytime needs while permitting the natural radiance of their own skin tone to shine through. Eyeshadow should be kept to a maximum of two shades for day, and for lips select a soft, natural-looking gloss or creme. At night, you might aim for a look that's bolder and a little more glamorous. Try a shimmery, iridescent shadow on your eyes, deeper blush, rosy lips, and painted fingernails. If you want to use fragrance, remember that less is more. Apply your perfume, cologne, or eau de toilette lightly on your throat, temples, and wrists. Learn to layer your scent. You might try using a scented bubble bath, talcum powder, and body lotion all in the same heady fragrance; then a light spray of cologne or a dab of perfume is all you need to complete the effect—and wait and see how it lasts! Another trick: In hot summer months try storing fragrances in the refrigerator; you'll feel cooled and refreshed when you spray them on.

Natural Beauty

All of us have a feature that we yearn to change. "If only my eyes were bigger . . ." laments Cathy, a pretty redhead. Bess of thick, dark tresses longs for straight, ash blonde hair. In most instances, however, these feelings reflect some deeper fear of insecurity about being popular and well liked by members of both sexes.

Unless there is a real need for cosmetic surgery, say a birth defect or an accident, no young person should contemplate so radical an option. Surgery is not a light or frivolous choice, but one that should be given years of thought before undertaking. If at age sixteen a girl "hates" her nose, she should wait until she is in her early to mid-twenties before deciding to alter her appearance under the surgeon's knife. More often than not, the desire to so drastically change one's appearance fades along with adolescent insecurities and doubts.

The same rule can be applied to other major changes such as dyeing your hair. Hair dye is both caustic and abrasive and can damage the hair's natural sheen and resilience. Usually what nature created is the most flattering and should be left at that. If you really have the urge for change, try henna or another subtle rinse to get the effect. A new haircut, if well done and stylish, can give you a whole new image of yourself.

Expanding Your Fashion Sense

While you don't want your role models to be inaccessible figures of wealth, fame, and glamour whose looks (and lives, at least at present) have little to do with your own, you can profit enormously by studying and learning from a variety of sources all around you.

Find yourself a fashion consultant. That may be a family member or a friend, and it needn't be someone of the same sex. Some older brothers have a wonderful flair for fashion and can help a little sister make the transition from tomboy to prom queen by their helpful comments and suggestions.

You may find yourself drawn to someone whose style intrigues you because it has a certain little *je ne sais quoi* that distinguishes it from a hundred other nice but essentially conventional looks.

Does your favorite cousin always manage to do something a bit offbeat with her hair, wear an unexpected but great little pin on her dress or jacket, select unusual color combinations? Persuade her to let you in on some of her secrets. Maybe you could plan a shopping trip or even a trip through your own closet to mix and match some old items for a new and exciting look.

Learn from a pro. When really in doubt, seek professional advice. Sometimes department stores offer a complimentary makeup lesson with a purchase. That can be a way of getting some beauty tips from an expert. You can learn how to accentuate your good features, conceal your bad ones, and choose flattering colors and shades.

Think of other professional services as well: Can the person who cuts your hair advise you about different coiffure styles? Can you learn to give yourself a professional manicure by having one in a salon the first time and then doing it yourself at home?

Don't underestimate the power of the printed word on this subject: Consult books written by experts on fashion, makeup, exercise, and posture. Read magazines, study pictures. Is there a salesperson whose advice you trust? The sources are endless. Don't be afraid to learn and keep learning. Pretty soon you may find that you've attracted a little following of your own and that people are coming to *you* for advice.

What to Wear When

It is impossible to provide a complete and totally accurate guide for dressing in every situation. For every rule, you can always find an exception. What follows establishes some general rules; study them and then take it from there.

At Home

Anything goes! Most families are pretty informal about how they look at home. But if your family dresses for dinner or special occasions, you should, too. When you have company, make the effort to change your shirt, comb your hair; guests deserve some sense of being special.

At School

Many schools are lenient these days about dress codes. Gone are the days of jackets and ties for boys, skirts for girls. Now, torn jeans and tee-shirts seem to become the norm.

Nonetheless, you should make an effort to appear attractive and well groomed at school. It affects the way your teachers look at you, and you want them to look at you in a positive light. Boys should wear clean, pressed clothes: slacks and a shirt or sweater; not a tee-shirt, and jeans only if they are new or freshly ironed. Girls too may wear jeans or slacks, although it wouldn't hurt your image to walk into your math class in a nice skirt and sweater. But remember that ultrahigh heels, low necklines, daring slits, and the like are better saved for parties. School is not the place for such eye-catching attire.

Makeup should be natural-looking, as should the style of your hair. Keep it off your face in the classroom; a covered elastic, pretty barrettes, or a headband can accomplish that.

Parties

"When in Rome . . ." If you're going to be with your friends, it is fine to let the situation dictate your choice of clothes. If it's a casual crowd, go in jeans. If the party is to be more formal, dress accordingly.

Parties to which you are invited with family members, however, are different. If on Thanksgiving at Aunt Sally's house Mom wants you to wear a dress or a suit jacket, you should accommodate her wishes.

On the Job

Dress depends very much on what kind of job you have. Cleaning swimming pools will require a different style of dress than working as a waitress or in a bank. Let the situation—and your boss—determine how you dress.

Dressing for the Future

Youth is a time of experimentation, a time of new modes of self-expression, a time of discovering an identity. As has been discussed, clothes play a vital part in it. In that context, there is no reason not to try any wild outfit you can imagine and follow the fickle winds of fashion. One season features leather pants, supple suede tunics, and jackets; another shows tie-tyed fabrics and Indian batiks. South American embroidery, Navaho turquoise, vampy dresses from the forties, and spandex pants from the eighties have all had their moment in the sun. Provided these kinds of clothes suit you and you like them, there is no reason not to indulge—at least sometimes. But if your budget is somewhat limited, you can get a lot more fashion mileage from a few good-quality "classic" garments that can serve you well for a number of years.

Consider style, workmanship, and fabric in assessing a garment. Good classic choices are wool tweed or houndstooth blazer for boys and girls, long-sleeved button-down shirts, a camel's-hair coat, loafers. Boys might think of investing in a few pairs of well-cut slacks in a variety of neutral shades. Girls might want to own a combination of slacks and skirts in basic styles such as dirndl, A-line, and peasant for a number of attractive and classic looks.

Learn to mix and match. Consider the combinations you can come up with from the following: one pair of black wool pants, one black linen skirt, one cotton knit sweater-vest in a bright red, royal blue, yellow, or purple, and one white cotton turtleneck. On a chilly day, you might wear the skirt, the long-sleeved cotton top and the vest; a more casual look would substitute the pants for the skirt. When the weather was warmer, you could wear the skirt and the polo shirt with the sleeves rolled up, or even the vest and skirt alone. If you begin to think that way, you can maximize your outfits with a minimum of investment and so stretch your fashion dollars.

By learning to use your accessories well, the possibilities for extending your wardrobe are even greater. Don't underestimate what a few well-chosen pieces can do. Take our basic black linen skirt again: Teamed with a pretty silk shirt, beads, and high heels, it's a charming spring party look; worn with knee socks, white blouse, and cardigan, you have the perfect back-to-school fall outfit.

Think of the value of scarves and belts, hats and gloves to create a new look. Pretty and inexpensive nighttime looks can be imaginatively created from costume jewelry like ropes of imitation pearls and rhinestone necklaces, along with shiny barrettes or a little silk flower to tuck behind your ear.

Nor should those of the male sex ignore this advice: Young

men can benefit from the addition of similar "extras" to their wardrobe. Consider the impact of your tie: Silks are dressy and elegant; cotton and wool knits are sporty and casual. Two or three jackets or blazers can change the character of the same pair of slacks and button-down shirt. Good shoes and attractive belts can add a lot to your total look.

So by all means, feel free to be crazy and unpredictable in your manner of dress sometimes. Buy Swedish clogs, Japanese kimonos, athletic sneakers, a Victorian cape—but save some room in your closet for a few timeless classics that will see you through more than a season.

CHAPTER IV

*The Dating Game: Have Times
Really Changed?*

Everyone wants to be the most popular girl or boy in the class, to simply *look* at members of the opposite sex and have them instantly respond, and to have dates lined up for all the weekend nights for the next five years. Well, it's a nice fantasy to indulge in once in a while.

This chapter can't promise you a magic elixir or a secret potion that will help you command the attention of any and everyone, but it does offer a few more practical hints that can enable you to make the transition from dreary, stay-at-home Saturdays to a healthy number of fun-filled and exciting dates.

The Readiness Is All

A big question for many teens is, "When do I start to date?" The answer, quite simply, is "When you are ready." That may differ by a number of months or, in some cases, years. Some girls of thirteen and fourteen have scads of dates and a new heart throb every week; others at sixteen or seventeen are content to consider boys as "just friends" and have no romantic inclinations whatever. Whether you fall into one of those categories or any place in between really doesn't matter. You should continue to do what feels right for you and not succumb to pressure from either peers or parents.

Of course, your parents may feel that you are too young to begin dating. Try sitting down with them and discussing the issue in a rational and open fashion; it may impress them more than you think and induce them to entertain your point of view.

If they still refuse to allow it, however, you will have to postpone formal dating for a while and stick to more casual encounters with friends.

Where the Girls (or Boys) Are

When you have decided that you indeed are ready, willing, and able to begin dating, you have to have people whom you can date. That goes for girls as well as boys, for girls are no longer expected to be so passive in their dealings with the opposite sex.

Start with the most familiar and obvious places: your school and neighborhood. If you are eager to meet the cute boy across the street, invite him in for some home-baked cookies or brownies and a glass of milk. At school, a boy should feel free to approach a girl he knows from Italian class or through mutual friends, but he shouldn't feel limited to prior acquaintance. Perhaps he sees a pretty girl in the hall between classes. Although he doesn't know her, he should feel comfortable to walk over, fall into step with her, and start a conversation. It's best to be friendly without being pushy or aggressive. In other words, talk to her a bit and see if you can establish some kind of rapport *before* you ask her for a date.

Girls should feel free to approach boys they don't know, although it still may be a hard role for them to play. Remember that many boys are greatly flattered by the attention of an attractive and outgoing girl, and they are relieved that the burden of making the first move can sometimes be shared. But girls also have to remember that equality in matters of the heart doesn't mean going overboard. Just because you think you're making up for centuries of male chauvinism, it doesn't mean that you should confront a fellow and demand a date on the spot. That is exactly the kind of treatment that girls object to from boys: Why should you be so quick to incorporate it into your behavior?

Other places to meet members of the opposite sex are at school functions such as dances, football/baseball/basketball games, and parties at the homes of friends or relatives.

Meeting strangers is a bit more risky, especially for girls. Before you decide to accept a date with someone you've met at the movies or downtown, find out a little about him first. How old is he, where does he live and go to school, what are his interests? What he says is important, and so is how he says it; you must learn to be a judge of character in such an instance. If you do decide to accept a date with him, insist that he call for you at your home and then go to some public place. Never accept a ride from someone you have just met, and never, *never* hitchhike.

If you really have trouble meeting young people that you would like to date, you might ask a more socially adept friend or sibling to help by making some introductions. Big brothers can provide a great supply of interesting boys for a lonely freshman girl to meet, and your best friend Joe's steady girl may have a half dozen friends who would love for you to give them a call sometime.

Making the First Move

Times *have* changed. More and more girls are asking their male schoolmates for dates, and more and more boys are accepting. But in doing so, girls are learning something that boys have known for a long time: Making the first move is hard, and being rejected can be very painful. Keep in mind, however, that it is something that you can live with and even grow from. You need to risk something of yourself in order to gain something, in life in general, as well as in romance.

When asking for a date, try making your request specific rather than general and see if the response doesn't improve dramatically. For example, instead of shuffling over with your hands in your pockets and saying, "Gee Mary, how would you like to get together some night?" try standing up straight and saying in a confident, pleasant tone, "Mary, I have two tickets to a concert on Thursday night; would you like to go with me?" The more specific you are, the more authoritative and self-assured you sound, and let's face it, self-assurance (not arrogance!) is sexy to anyone. So learn to ask very particular and focused questions, and your batting average is bound to improve.

The First Date

So you've actually gone ahead and made the date, the time has rolled around, and now you're standing on the front steps of your house, about to set off to meet . . . HER. Only your stomach is in knots and your palms are soaking wet: What can you do to calm yourself down?

Everyone gets first-date jitters, so try to remember that they are no more than normal. Will he/she like me? Will we have anything to say to each other? What if I have a terrible time? Will he/she ever want to see me again? Those questions and more are apt to be floating through your mind, making you hopelessly nervous.

Tell yourself that if this person asked you out on a date or agreed to go on one with you, he or she already has some positive feelings about you. Just try to relax and be the person that you are—the person who was asked out on this date or accepted it. Be friendly and warm, and your companion will like you even better by the time the evening is over. Talk about things that really interest you rather than things you think will impress. Ask questions, and be sure to listen to the answers; half of being a good conversationalist is knowing how to listen. On the other hand, gone are the days when boys did all the talking while girls sat meek and mute. Nowadays, equal time is the name of the game, so make sure that you know how to play.

A Few Basic Rules

First dates can make everyone jumpy, and you want so much to make a good impression that it becomes hard to relax and respond naturally to the situation. Here are a few hints to get things moving along and have that special person look forward to your *next* date with pleasure.

On a first date, it is appropriate for a boy to pick up a girl at her house. Later on, you may agree to meet at the home of a friend, the movies, or the pizza shop, but for the first time you should observe this small formality. A polite girl greets her date herself; that means being ready *on time*. Don't keep your date waiting, chewing his nails and trying to make conversation with your kid sister, before you even know the guy! Introduce him to your parents, too. In short, if you look forward to a second and third date with this young man, it's a good idea to attend to his comfort and ease on the first one.

Be a gentleman. Even if you think it's old-fashioned and silly, it never fails to impress. It means that you have manners and that you care. So open doors for her, help her on and off with her coat, slide her chair out at the restaurant, take her arm crossing the street. It's the little extras like those that get you noticed—and remembered—in the right way.

Few girls expect gifts from their dates these days, but on a first date flowers or candy are traditional and appropriate. On a formal date, such as a school dance, buy her a corsage. Be sure to ask the color of the dress she is planning to wear. Red roses are lovely, but not when worn with a bright fuchsia dress.

Confirm your plans. On a first date it is considerate to call the evening before and go over again the time you are to meet. If anything comes up that changes or postpones your plans, you do the other person the courtesy of enabling him or her to change the schedule accordingly.

Be kind. Even if you realize within the first fifteen minutes that you and your date have nothing in common and probably will never see each again, you are obliged for the evening. That means trying to hold a conversation and being polite. There is no excuse for rude behavior. Don't ignore your date or pay too much attention to someone you may have met at a party or social gathering. Feel free to talk with others, but do not leave your date for any reason. To do so demonstrates lack of consideration and immature thoughtlessness—not traits that you want to cultivate in your personality.

Who Pays for What?

It used to be that the male partner paid for everything. In these times of changing male and female roles, however, things are a little more complex. Some girls don't like their date to pay for everything; it makes them feel obligated to please and dependent on the other person. Other girls feel that if a boy asks them out on a date, it is his responsibility to foot the bill. There is no one right answer anymore.

Generally, it is still the mark of a gentleman to pay for a lady, especially when he is first getting to know her. After a few dates you may suggest going Dutch, and a gracious girl occasionally offers to pay her own way. If that idea really bothers you, you can always make a nice supper for a boy who has taken you out several times; it's a lovely way to reciprocate and sure to be appreciated.

Where Do We Go?

Lots of teens complain that they are bored with their leisure-time routine of movies and television, television and movies, a pattern broken only by an occasional party or get-together with friends. If that sounds like you, why not suggest something a bit more unusual on your next date? It doesn't have to be fancy or expensive to impress the other person with your creativity and imagination. Following are a few date ideas that depart slightly from the beaten path.

The Zoo or the Aquarium. How long has it been since you've seen the lions and monkeys, or the seals and baby whales? Wouldn't it be fun to have a companion when you visit them? Be sure to take your camera along.

A long bicycle ride. Get your bike out of the garage or basement, borrow one from a friend, or even rent a tandem! Bicycle riding is fun for two, especially if you've packed a picnic lunch of sandwiches, chips, cookies, and fruit. Pedal away and enjoy!

Breakfast. How about making a date for the early morning hours when most people are still asleep or at home in their robes? One weekend morning, meet your date early enough to hear the birds still twittering and head for a diner to have eggs and bacon or a pancake house for some steaming flapjacks dripping with butter and maple syrup.

Botanical gardens. Does your town or one nearby have formal public gardens? Take along a guidebook so that you can name the flowers and shrubs, and let your nose lead you along.

Flea markets or garage sales. Try searching for interesting old books and records or hidden treasures at a local flea market. You might come up with a valuable antique. Don't overlook craft fairs; handmade items can be found at bargain prices, so stock up for Christmas.

Try some culture. Are there museums in your area worth visiting? Think of other things besides paintings: restored houses, aviation, history, and the like can provide interesting and stimulating conversation, both while you're there and for some time to come.

Amusement parks. Another often neglected spot for those over the age of ten. You probably haven't been to one for years, but now is the time to go again and take a date. Be sure to have at least one ride on the roller coaster, stop for franks, popcorn, or cotton candy, have your picture taken in a funny costume, and reach for the brass ring on the carousel.

If you learn to free your imagination and your expectations, you may be pleasantly surprised. Sometimes it's easier to open up and enjoy the company of a date if you remove yourselves from the commonplace dating conventions of your peers.

What Should I Wear?

Although the matter of dress and clothing was dealt with in

Chapter III, dressing for a date is often a sticky business and deserves some special attention.

First, you need to find out in advance where you are going and what you are going to do. As a general rule, it is better to be slightly underdressed than overdressed. Nothing can make you feel sillier or more out of place than a fancy dress and high-heeled shoes at a casual restaurant or an informal gathering. Learn to look neat, attractive, and smartly dressed with a minimum of fussing.

The one situation, however, in which it is hard to be overdressed is a formal occasion such as a dance, prom, or wedding.

The Formal Affair—for Him

Think about wearing a tuxedo. You may prefer to rent one for the evening rather than investing in one of your own or borrowing one from a friend. Renting has the advantage of letting you select a garment that really fits and looks well on you. If you don't wear a tuxedo, a dark suit is in order, either black or very dark blue.

Tails are extremely formal attire, so be sure that the occasion warrants them.

With your tux or suit, you should wear an impeccable light-colored shirt—white is always best. Remember that a soiled or wrinkled shirt is worse than no shirt at all—be scrupulously neat! Well-shined shoes, neat tie (either bow or regular), attractive belt or cummerbund—all these details add up to an appearance of polished elegance. You might even wear a caranation in your lapel for a special touch.

In the winter or in cool weather, choose a sober dark topcoat over your tuxedo or suit—not your orange ski parka, please! For the summer months, a white tuxedo is an extremely elegant formal evening costume.

The Formal Affair—for Her

For girls, formal wear still means a long dress, although you can attend many important dressy affairs in an elegant street-length dress. Evening slacks of silk or velvet are sometimes worn, but check whether pants are appropriate attire.

A formal gown should be flattering in its cut and fit and should suit both you and the occasion. Keep in mind that while black is lovely and eye-catching, it is too severe for a young girl. Stick to pastels or white, although white is not appropriate at a wedding—you don't want to upstage the bride. If you insist on black, try a floor-length black evening skirt in some wonderful fabric like taffeta, satin, or velvet and team it up with a pretty blouse. White is always attractive, but consider red for holiday wear, or pale pink, mauve, turquoise, lavender, or a bright shade of blue or purple.

Strapless dresses or gowns with daring slits can be very appealing but should not be worn to a wedding or any conservative affair. An alternative is to wear a small stole or evening jacket over your strapless dress for a more discreet and covered-up look.

Young women and girls also tend to look overdressed in furs. Wait a few more years for your mink stole or wrap. Think instead of a fur-trimmed coat or a fur hat or muff as elegant outside evening wear in the colder months.

Shoes should be attractive and graceful; pumps and evening sandals in satin, velvet, brocade, or patent leather. If you opt for heels, make sure that you can walk and dance in them too, if the situation arises. It would be a pity to turn down Prince Charming because your feet were killing you.

Gloves are not required these days but can still look very chic when worn with a gown. Makeup should be bright and festive but not overpowering. Flowers—worn in the hair, on the wrist, or pinned to the bodice as a corsage—are perhaps the most beautiful adornment for any nighttime look.

Think carefully about jewelry. Too little at your age is far better than too much. Wear a single strand of pearls or a pair of fabulous diamond studs—and no other pieces. It will make an attractive and elegant statement. If you don't own any good jewelry, think about asking for something at Christmas or on your birthday.; you are getting to an age when it's nice to begin collecting it. If all else fails, perhaps your mother or older sister can lend you something for that special night. Make sure the clasps and hooks are secure, though, before you go flitting away in your borrowed finery!

The Stirrings of Romance

Let's say you've made it past the hurdle of asking someone out, the anxiety of the first date, and even a second and a third. By that time, you really start relaxing and having a good time with this person, and you look forward to your dates with a special kind of glow.

At a certain point, you start to get moony and starry-eyed. You daydream in class, doodle his or her name all over your school books, run to the telephone every time it starts to ring. Your friends wonder what's the matter with you, and your parents shake their heads indulgently and sigh. The signs are all there: You're in love.

Adolescent love can be one of the most exhilarating experiences possible. Never before have you been so happy or felt such bliss. You're walking on air all the time. But teenage love can be fraught with anxiety and pain, too. You may not be ready for the full weight of responsibility that loving someone carries with it. And to counteract these feelings, you may tend to cling tightly to your "beloved" and cut yourself off from other important contacts.

Going steady does have its advantages: You always have someone to count on, Saturday nights are a sure thing, and there is the real warmth and affection you feel for each other. In the first throes of love you may want nothing more than to commit yourself utterly to the other person.

Katy, an attractive and bright fifteen-year-old, spends most of her time with Jim, her boyfriend of six months. Since they go to school together, they have ample time to enjoy each other's company, but Katy goes even further and refuses other dates and ignores her friends. When she's not with Jim, she daydreams about him constantly. She imagines that one night he'll take off his heavy class ring and slip it on her delicate ring finger, where it dangles loosely. She smiles but doesn't meet his eyes, fingering the heavy gold ornament. "I'll have to get a chain to wear this around my neck," she tells him. Maybe one day, and she hopes that it will be soon, he'll exchange that class ring for a simple band that has at its center one perfect, sparkling diamond.

Katy is not unusual, and there is nothing wrong with her fantasies. But at fifteen, is she really ready to select a mate for life?

Adolescence is a time when you are free to experiment and broaden your social and emotional horizons. Going steady may inhibit that important process. Of course, no one can insist that you change your feelings, but going steady in your teens may have serious repercussions in later life. Your ability to select and fall in love with an appropriate partner and eventually marry and have a family is based in part on the scope of your teenage experiences. You need to meet many kinds of people before you can fully understand your own expectations and desires.

Try to keep things in perspective. Don't buy each other expensive gifts, for instance, for they suggest seriousness and permanence that are not yet appropriate. Don't insist on taking your boyfriend or girlfriend to all family functions; he or she is not yet a part of the intimate family circle. Having a favorite boy or girl friend is fine, but try not to let that feeling limit you before you've had a chance to really expand and grow.

Sex—the Big Question

It has been said that the onset of puberty and the subsequent sexual awakening that it brings represent one of the greatest crises in the human life cycle. Certainly the shift from childhood into adolescence is an important change, celebrated by rites of passage as diverse as a confirmation, a bar mitzvah, or ritual scarification.

Sex and sexuality are extremely significant aspects of our adult lives, and it is true that in the beginning these new feelings and ways of behaving can cause a teenager much awkwardness and embarrassment.

Ignorance Is Not Bliss

Perhaps the largest single factor contributing to the awkwardness teens feel about sex is the general air of mystery with which it is shrouded. No one seems to want to tell you anything about it, and surely you can't be expected to know everything by yourself.

"X" ratings bar teens from movies, older people change the subject or speak in euphemisms when sex comes up, and it becomes the focus of all kinds of vague, uninformed, and often distorted fantasies. Added to that, many adolescents feel their own lack of experience as shameful and indulge in bragging about fictitious exploits to conceal their true innocence.

Before you make any decisions, you need to become informed. Most teens in this day and age are reasonably aware of the basic facts of life—increasingly liberal attitudes and sex education in schools have contributed that much—but that may be all they know. They may have all kinds of questions about what is normal behavior as well as concerns about pregnancy and venereal disease. If your school does not offer sex education and your parents will not answer your questions honestly and openly, try to find someone who will. It should be a person whom you trust and who will respect the confidential and sensitive nature of the topic. Perhaps an older sibling, a cousin, or a friend of the family could help, or you might turn to a minister, priest, or rabbi for advice. Don't be ashamed of what you don't know. People are born into this world ignorant socially, sexually, intellectually, and all you can do is learn.

How Far Should I Go?

That is a very delicate and personal decision and not one that you should treat lightly. Teachers, parents, religious leaders can all try to guide and influence you, but ultimately the choice is your own.

For that reason, don't let anyone—not your date, your steady boyfriend, your friends at school—pressure you into doing something that you don't want or aren't ready to do.

You may want to stop at a good-night kiss, or you may want to involve yourself in a more intimate and serious way. But you are entitled to make up your own mind about what you want, so you need to have the courage to stick to it. Do something only because *you* want to, not because someone else is urging you to participate.

Sometimes that means removing yourself from temptation. If you are alone with a boy in a parked car, overlooking a tranquil pond glittering with moonlight, and he begins to pressure you for a kiss or a caress, you *can* say "No." But "No" is awfully difficult to say and mean if you continue to sit there with him; after all, you are both only human. Instead, have him drive you home, and think twice before allowing the same situation to occur again.

Boys in our culture are taught to be aggressive and assertive when it comes to getting what they want, including sexual favors. Girls may admire strength and forcefulness in their male companions, but a boy should never let his behavior turn brutal or menacing. There is an ugly word for boys who try to force girls to do things that they don't want to do. Real men don't coerce anyone. Consider the wishes of your girlfriend or date with the same care you would give your own. If you persist in ignoring them, you may find that you've lost a friend.

Breaking a Date

As a general principle, don't break dates that you have made. If you have agreed to the date, you should make every effort to keep it. If you really don't want to spend time with this particular person, don't agree to the date in the first place.

Many times we are tempted to say "Yes" to someone because we don't want to hurt his or her feelings. That is a poor reason to accept a date. No one likes to be pitied, and in the end you do more harm than good by raising someone's hopes, only to dash them later on. Far better to say "No" gently but firmly at the outset than to endure a boring or uncomfortable evening. In fact, learning to say "No" is an important social skill. It may be unpleasant and difficult at times, but the alternatives are far worse. Learn to do it now, and you will find it very useful later on.

If, however, you have a legitimate excuse, such as illness, schoolwork, or family obligations, you can break the date. Call the other person early so as not to leave him or her stranded on a Saturday night, and try to suggest alternative plans then and there.

In that way he or she won't feel that you've simply changed your mind or received a more exciting offer at the last minute. "I'm sorry I can't make it tonight, Brenda, but could you go to the movies with me on Thursday instead?" does a lot to ease anyone's misgivings about a sudden change of plans. Remember that constantly breaking dates can give you a bad reputation with your friends, and you may find yourself without *any* dates if you persist in doing it.

A Bad Date

Every now and then you will run into a situation that seems impossible to salvage. Your date is late, is dressed poorly, is rude to your mother, talks too much or not at all—what should you do?

First, you need to examine what is really going on and decide if it holds any potential danger. A date who monopolizes the conversation all evening long may be a bore but will probably not harm you. Endure it as best you can and resolve to reject any future invitations. But a date who has had too much to drink and is responsible for driving you home is another matter entirely. If you are at a party or with a group of friends, you can discreetly ask someone else to drive you home. You can tell your date privately of your decision, and if he objects, be polite but don't give in. It's your safety that's at stake. If, however, you are out alone, you might offer to drive yourself. If all else fails, call home. Your parents will be only too happy to help out in such a situation, and they will certainly applaud your common sense and good judgment.

As a general rule, then, you should try to tolerate any behavior that is annoying but not harmful or damaging. That includes emotional damage as well as physical; no one should endure a date who becomes verbally abusive or hostile. The implicit contract you made is violated when the other person insults you in any way. Feel free to end the evening early.

Breaking Up Is Hard to Do

There is a special kind of sadness attached to the end of a romance, no matter how brief it may have been. It always hurts to say good-bye and to relinquish the fond feelings and tender memories. But keep in mind that all romances ultimately have only two options: either the partners choose to marry and spend the rest of their lives together, or at some point, whether it be in six months or six years, they must part company.

Sometimes parting is a natural and relatively painless process. A boy or girl you have been seeing for several months goes off to college or moves to another town. At first you feel lonely and miss each other terribly, but gradually you both begin to meet others and the pain of your separation is diminished. You may even find someone you prefer to the earlier romantic figure. That is a natural part of your growth and development, and you should accept it as such.

Even when the break-up is more traumatic, such as when one partner finds someone else, you must try to retain some perspective on it. At fourteen, fifteen, or sixteen, it is highly unlikely that you will find your lifelong mate. It is ultimately better to have had experiences with many kinds of people before you settle down.

Don't forget the old adage: 'Tis better to have loved and lost than never to have loved at all. Although it has become a cliché, it is nonetheless true. The ability to love another human being is something that is alive within you. Even if you lose that person, your capacity for loving remains intact. It may be bruised and sore for a while, but it doesn't vanish and it doesn't die. When enough time has elapsed and you have begun to heal, you will find that the stirrings of new love can be as sweet as the old, if not sweeter.

CHAPTER V

Preparing for Adulthood: Jobs and Careers

Beginning your first job is always an exciting and memorable event, like your graduation from high school, or your engagement. Sometimes you'll have a lucky break: Your favorite uncle owns a clothing store and wants you to help out behind the counter, or your father's office needs a temporary clerk to help out with the phones, typing, and filing. But there are other times when you look for work and have more difficulty. You diligently scout out all the ads in the local papers, ask everyone you know, and still you have no luck. What can you do to increase your chances for success?

Well, it depends on what kind of position you are seeking. Perhaps you are a high school sophomore who wants summer work to earn spending money for going to the movies and out for pizza with your friends. You aren't ready to choose a career, nor should you be; your main goal is to get through the summer. But you still need not waste valuable time waiting for a job to fall into your lap. There's a lot you can do right now to land the job you want. You've looked through the want ads, you say; OK, that's a start. But what about advertising *yourself*? Can you mow lawns, paint houses, groom animals, prepare gourmet delicacies, wash a car? All of those skills can be lucrative if you let people know you have them. The services you can render to people are as limitless and far-reaching as your imagination, so let yourself go!

Put up signs in local stores and on community bulletin boards. If you have a particular talent such as exquisite French, think about taking out a small ad in the local paper. Or be really creative and design a flyer or leaflet that you can leave in neighborhood banks and stores. The point is to go out and find your market, not to lose time waiting for it to come to you. And when you do begin to get customers, ask them for referrals to spread the word of your services. If you're good, they'll be happy to help you out, and thus you can avail yourself of some free advertising.

But perhaps you are looking for a different kind of job, one that is more career-oriented and may be a stepping-stone toward your adult life. In that case you have to employ a slightly different approach. In the grownup, professional world, the résumé is the standard job-seeking tool. Everyone should have a résumé, and even though yours will change considerably over the next few years, it will be to your advantage to gain some experience in preparing one. Résumé forms vary; consult your library's career section for books that give samples. Note the information included: full name, address, telephone numbers where you can be reached during business hours, work experience, schooling, related interests, hobbies, skills, and any awards or honors that you may have received. You may also want to include the names of persons who can be contacted as references, although that is not mandatory.

Remember that your résumé reflects directly on *you*. If it is sloppy and filled with misspellings and typographical errors, it does not represent you in your best light. The form you present to the world does count, and you should take great care in its preparation. Your résumé should be neat, typed on good paper, and easy to read. If you can't do the proper job typing it yourself, see if you can enlist the help of a friend or relative. If need be, you can have it professionally done. At your stage that is not necessary, but if you do decide to spend the money, think of it as an investment in yourself and your future.

The Interview

After you've sent out résumés in response to interesting advertisements you've seen, or simply to companies for which you feel you might like to work, you may be called for an interview. That is the next step in the job search, and it is an important one. Many people are nervous before an interview, but there is no need for it if you are fully prepared. Handling an interview is a great skill to learn early, and one that will serve you well all of your adult life.

Even if the meeting is to be brief, the person interviewing you will be judging and evaluating, finding reasons to accept or reject you, so you should learn *now* how to tip the balance in your favor.

Punctuality

Punctuality is a virtue in any social context, and it is even more important in a professional one. Potential employers place great weight on an applicant's ability to be prompt, and one can hardly blame them. If you can't be on time when you're trying to make a good impression, what can your future employer expect on a daily basis? Being late means that you just don't care, and that's not the attitude you want to convey. So make every effort to be at your appointment on time. Plan your route if you're heading toward an unfamiliar neighborhood; prepare your clothes in advance; wake up early enough (and don't forget to have a good breakfast!). Better to have fifteen or twenty minutes to spare than to race in overheated and out of breath.

Do Your Homework

Be prepared for your interview. That can mean a number of things. Is there someone you can talk to about the company? Is there some material you can read in advance? While you're waiting for your interviewer, use the time to read any brochures, leaflets, or other promotional information that may be distributed in the reception area. When your interviewer asks you questions, you should have a little background.

Think about your goals and objectives: Why are you applying

to this particular company or agency? If it's a large architectural firm, and you're an aspiring architect, the answer is obvious. But if it's a real estate firm and you're not sure what you want to do with the rest of your life, you might reflect a bit on what specifically drew you to this position. Does the job involve a good deal of telephone work, and you know yourself to be naturally gregarious and outgoing? Is there much detailed figure work, and you're a math whiz? Whatever it is, think about it, so that you can emphasize it in the interview.

Dressing for Success

This topic is covered more extensively in Chapter III, but it is not inappropriate to say a few words about it in this context.

A job interview is one place where your creativity and fashion flair are out of place. Unless you are seeking a job in a glamorous fashion firm, wild colors and daring styles are definitely not in order. Save them for your after-hours fun. Instead, you should appear at your most conservative and dignified.

For boys, a suit is essential. Even in the summer, there is nothing as pulled together or as polished looking as a good suit. Wear the vest if you wish, although it is no longer mandatory. Don't spoil the look with unshined shoes or a wrinkled shirt. All the pieces should be as perfect as you can make them.

For girls, a suit is equally appropriate, although you can wear a skirt and coordinated (not matching) blazer, or a good dress with a blazer. Avoid clothing that is too brightly colored or patterned: red, hot pink, and orange should be passed up in favor of more neutral tones. Skip the high heels, slits, and plunging neckline; this is a job interview, not prom night.

One final word about interviewing: You are also sizing up the company and forming some opinions of your own, even though you're doing it more discreetly. Don't forget that this is a good time for you to get a sense of your prospective boss before you've committed yourself to the job. Is he or she polite to you? Is the interview riddled with unnecessary interruptions? Does he or she appear to be genuinely interested in your potential growth? All of these questions can help you to evaluate the situation you may be on the verge of entering.

Rules of the Game

Once you've obtained a job, be it as a summer secretary in a publishing company or pruning the shrubbery at the local nursery, there are certain general rules of conduct to which you should try to adhere.

Be punctual! That cannot be overemphasized. Nothing annoys a boss or co-worker more than someone who is chronically tardy. The habit labels you as unreliable and immature. Learn the value of punctuality *now*, and let it be a lesson that you remember well.

Dress. Here you should take your cue from others around you. If the office is one in which even your boss wears jeans, it is all right for you to wear them too. Most offices, however, require more formal attire. Of course, if you're in doubt, you can always ask.

Even if you're selling ice cream cones from a wagon on the street, you should make the effort to be neat, clean, and presentable—especially if you are handling food.

If you're engaged in construction work or painting houses, however, this particular rule can be overlooked.

Office Politics. This is a term used to describe the dynamics of your job situation that hold possible dangers and pitfalls. Remember that although the people you work with may become your friends, they usually don't start out that way, and you should always consider the working relationship first. Be friendly and open, but be circumspect as well. Don't reveal all your romantic woes to a co-worker with whom you are not very close just because you need a willing ear; it may come back to you in a very unpleasant way. Better to wait until you're near a phone and can call a trusted friend.

If possible, stay out of office quarrels and feuds; they're a complication that you don't need. Avoid damaging and cruel gossip, too.

Your workplace may indeed be the source of some close and wonderful friendships, but you need to proceed a little more slowly here than you would somewhere else. That is a good rule to learn early in life. Too many adults try to mix business and pleasure and end up failing at both.

Odd Jobs

Even if the work you've found is informal and less routinized, there are still ways to think of yourself as a professional and expect to be treated as such. For instance, if you've agreed to mow a neighbor's lawn, decide on the fee beforehand, based on your expectations of the difficulty of the work and the time it will take you to complete. You may set the fee by the hour or by the job; the choice is yours, and you should feel free to exercise if. Of course, you should avoid becoming too rigid in your stance; some flexibility is necessary to maintain the goodwill of your customers.

There are other situations in which your judgment and standards will come into play: If you tend pets, for instance, feeding a canary is less work than walking, bathing, and playing with two frisky pups; putting two coats of paint on a wall requires more effort than one. Are you going to charge a client for materials used in the completion of a task; if so, let him or her know that in advance. Do you want to join forces with a friend? Decide early on how you want to divide up the responsibilities — and the profits. All these things can get you thinking in a "professional" way and will be a help to you in your later career ventures.

Preparing for Your Future

Summer work is one thing; the extra money that it brings in is nice, and the experience, say, of being a swimming counselor at a lakeside camp is the stuff of which fond memories are woven. But what about working while you're still in school in any way that may help you grow into a career?

Most teens do start to work fairly young on an informal basis, as we've touched upon here: They do chores, take care of kids, wait tables in their spare time. But there may be a way for you to channel your creative energies into a more directed path. This is a time when you might consult your guidance counselor. Does your school offer work-study courses, for which you could get credit for field work done outside the classroom? Maybe your aptitude with young children can extend beyond baby-sitting and can land you a job assisting in a kindergarten. Perhaps your school could give you credit for the work you've done after you've written a paper that analyzes and evaluates the experience. That in turn could help you in applying for some future job or getting into college. Are there other opportunities that you can create for yourself? Although you are young and shouldn't be burdened with complete financial responsibility for yourself, you can still do a lot now to prepare and shape your future course in life.

CHAPTER VI

The Written Word

It's a fact that people don't write as much as they used to. We live, after all, in an age of high technology and sophisticated electronic equipment. We have tape recorders and radios; it takes only moments to dial a number across the Atlantic and speak to Paris, London, Rome, or Madrid. We have cameras that can take a picture and develop it in sixty seconds, giant television screens, and devices that can record shows for us when we're not at home and play them back when we are. The net result of all this is that people are lazier about writing; they almost feel they can afford to be because they don't have to do it so often. And the less they do it, the harder it becomes to do. Pretty soon it's a chore, and then people stop writing at all.

As a young person growing up in the midst of this technological paradise you should do everything you can to develop and perfect your writing skills. Writing is a key to language, history, and culture, and you should not lock yourself out. This chapter is designed to help you deal with a few situations in which you are required to find social expression through the written word.

Letter Writing—the Social Side

All of us love to receive mail, but how prompt are we in sending it? If you want to receive, you must first give. So learn, as rule number one, to answer promptly. Don't wait until three months have elapsed, by which time you are too embarrassed to pick up your pen and the correspondence withers and dies. Answer your friends and relatives quickly, and they will extend the same courtesy to you. If there is a reason, such as illness, for your failure to respond, don't let it deter you from resuming contact. Just be sure to express your apology at the beginning of the letter and try not to be so tardy next time.

When writing to friends and relatives, a hand-written note is preferable to a typed one. Write neatly, and use lined paper if you must, to keep your sentences from running into each other. You can use stationery that is either plain or fancy, but be sure that it isn't torn or dirty. Even a clean piece of ruled legal paper is preferable to a crumpled, soiled piece of the finest rag stationery. Some people have their name or address or both engraved or printed on their letter paper. It adds a personalized touch to correspondence.

Use a pen rather than a pencil. Ink is easier to read and is less likely to smudge when you fold it and place it in an envelope.

Letters to friends need not be formal in style or content. Rather than full-sized paper, small note cards enlivened by a picture or illustration are appropriate, and picture postcards are always a treat in anyone's mailbox.

The contents of your letters will, of course, vary according to your personality and that of the recipient. Your grandmother living in a distant town will expect (and should get) a different kind of letter than will your girlfriend who is spending the summer at camp. Your older sister can describe the same family vacation in Cape Cod and the result will be an entirely different letter. Nevertheless, some basic kinds of information can be used in letters of a personal nature.

The Weather. That may seem to be a cliché, but it is always a safe and easy way to start a letter, especially for someone who has trouble with the next sentence after "Dear Mom . . ."

Something You've Done Recently. Of course, if you're visiting Los Angeles or New York for the first time, you might have a lot more to write about than if you're at home in Iowa living your ordinary routine. But does that have to be true? Isn't there something unique and special you can impart to your reader just by the quality and details of your writing? Perhaps you went on what seemed like a very uneventful walk last night. But think again. Did you see an unusual bird, a beautiful bush in blossom, a new park being built, or an old, spooky house being torn down? Write about it. Did you meet anyone interesting or see someone who intrigued you? Was there anything exciting, sad, funny, surprising, lovely, or frightening that you encountered along the way? Those kinds of details (and the more the better) will make your description of commonplace events really come alive.

Read Any Good Books Lately? Again, that may seem like a cliché, but it doesn't have to be one. Try to express the more intellectual side of your nature. Are you reading a book that is very special? What about it makes it so compelling? Or have you seen a movie recently that you want to see over and over again? What scenes moved/scared/delighted you? Why? All of those observations can make for very interesting letters.

Gossip. Not the harmful, malicious kind that hurts feelings and ruins friendships, but gossip of a more innocent nature is always of interest to people. Is there a new play at the civic center? Is someone getting married, having a baby, moving away, being promoted? Everyone is curious about the doings of other people, especially people they know, and your letters will come alive through the idiosyncratic anecdotes that you relate.

Ask Questions. Not six or ten, all in a row; that tends to make your reader feel as if you don't care about the answers but just want to fill the blank page. Questions that reflect a real interest in and knowledge of the other person, however, are a different story. Remember to inquire about your aunt's rose garden, your cousin's new puppy, your best friend's tennis lessons. Questions make your reader feel special and attended to, and your letters will sparkle and glow with warmth.

These suggestions are intended to open your mind to the many possibilities for expression in letter writing and to loosen the cap on your pen. Your letters need not be works of art to be very meaningful to those who receive them. They need only be a warm and sincere expression of the person who wrote them— you.

The Professional Letter

This can be the letter you write to inquire about a job, college or university admission, or a course or training program. It may be a letter written to a newspaper or magazine to express an opinion on something you've read, or to a business to complain about service or a product. This letter has a specific public function and will be different in both form and content from personal letters.

If at all possible, beg, borrow, or steal a typewriter or hire someone who can do it for you, but type your professional letters! Typing is the universal language in an adult world. Typing means, quite simply, business. There is no better way to ensure that your letter will be treated seriously and given the attention it deserves, so you should acquire this habit early and stick with it. Of course, if you are stranded without a typewriter at 11:30 one night in a blizzard, and the letter *must* be postmarked by midnight . . . you can always go ahead and write it by hand, printed clearly in dark ink on lined or unlined paper. But barring such circumstances, opt for the typewritten, not the written, word.

Skip the fancy stationery, too. No shocking pink or skyblue paper, glow-in-the-dark decals, or artful doodles that are the envy and delight of all your friends. Instead, select plain white bond paper (the heavier it is, the better the quality—and the impression that you make) or a subtle shade of gray, beige, or blue. Be sure to include your address in the upper right-hand corner.

Business letters, unlike personal ones, should be short and to the point. This is not the place for you to experiment with flowing elegant prose. Use simple and uncomplicated sentences that let you get right to the heart of the matter. Your reader should know by the very first sentence why this letter is being sent to him or her.

As for form, you might consult your library. Some books suggest indentation; others the block form. Either one is correct, but you should be consistent. The letter should include the name and address of the person to whom it is addressed, as well as your own address and the date. End your letter with a standard closing, such as "Yours truly" or "Sincerely." Your name should be typed underneath your signature—which should, by the way, be written in blue or black ink, not with a red felt-tipped pen.

Cards

Greeting cards have become extremely popular and they have become pretty specialized, too. You can buy a Valentine's Day card for your grandmother, a Mother's Day card for the mother of your best friend, an anniversary card for your parents, grandparents, sister and brother-in-law, cousins, or friends. Certainly, there is no reason not to send cards to the people you care for. The attractive pictures and drawings and tender or witty sayings have helped to make the greeting card industry what it is today. But printed cards can be slightly impersonal, so why not add a line or two of your own to the message, to convey a little of your spirit to the recipient? It need not be much—just a sentence or two that is clearly from you will make your card stand out among the rest.

Thank-yous

This subject was discussed earlier, so let this act as a reminder. Thank-you notes have all but gone out of fashion except for wedding and baby gifts. This is one area where you can afford, and even strive, to be old-fashioned. Nothing speaks better of your manners, breeding, and personality than a short note expressing thanks for the thoughtfulness of a birthday gift or that of a generous host.

Condolences

As a young person, your need for writing a condolence message will be limited. But in the sad event that you must do it, remember that it is an important and meaningful custom. At a time of loss and grief, your simple, straightforward message can act as balm to those who are feeling the pain of bereavement. They will appreciate the gesture, and it will make them feel less alienated and alone. You can buy a card and add a line of your own, or simply use a piece of plain stationery on which to write your message.

It is hoped that these suggestions will get you into some good letter-writing habits. Who knows, you may find it such fun that you will find yourself a pen pal through one of the numerous clubs, just so that you can have another friend with whom to correspond. The poet John Donne wrote, "Letters mingle souls." Let your pen be a way for you to begin a new and potentially rich, rewarding friendship.

CHAPTER VII

College-bound

Congratulations! You've finally done it—made your way through the maze of catalogues and applications, fretted over test scores and results—and now you have been accepted by the college of your choice. You're eager and excited, counting the days until your departure for school, but you're also just a little bit scared. What will the next four years bring? Many changes, to be sure, and those years will really mark your passage from the world of being a child to that of adulthood. You will become many things in the next few years and encounter many new people and experiences. Finding your way may be a bit tough at first, so try to sail off into the unknown waters with as much knowledge and preparation as possible.

Before You Leave

If you haven't visited your college or university yet, now is most certainly the time for you to do it. Plan a weekend with Mom or Dad or even your best friend, and get a firsthand look at this new place that you are going to be calling home. A visit gives you the opportunity to observe and to meet students who are presently enrolled. You want to get a sense of college life. How do people dress? What is the weather like? How spread out is the campus? What kind of social activities are common to the student body? Winters in Minnesota will call for down jackets and ski boots; those spent in Florida on the other hand will require such gear as swimming trunks, snorkel, and flippers. On some college campuses, jeans and flannel shirts are the uniform; others still have eating clubs where boys need a jacket and tie to be admitted.

When you visit, do your best to watch other students and draw conclusions from what you see. Don't be shy. If the college offers a tour of the campus and its buildings be sure that you're on it. Look at bulletin boards that announce social and recreational events, and read the school newspaper. Being prepared will do much to take the edge off your predeparture jitters.

Don't forget that many schools sponsor get-togethers such as teas or lunches for new and prospective students in your own home town or nearby. Find out if your school offers such activities, and perhaps you can even kindle some new friendships before you've left home.

Living Accommodations

Pay attention to your living arrangements; they will either add to or subtract from your experience at school, and they may have a direct influence on your grades and your social life. Many options exist for today's college students, and gone are the days of single-sex dormitories and strict rules and parietals. Colleges tend to be more lenient, and hence the need for more caution and foresight on your part: You will have to rely more on yourself to get what you want. You want to make the best choice possible and so enhance your time at school, especially during your first year, which is filled with so many changes and upheavals.

Dorm Life

Living in a dormitory is another area that may require advance preparation. Carefully fill out any forms or questionnaires that you are sent prior to your first semester, and be prompt in sending them back. Do you want to live in a dorm that is coeducational or single-sex—often there is a choice. Would you like to take your dog with you? Are you a stickler about quiet? Many of these are options that will be open to you if you act early enough.

You may be given a room to yourself, but more often than not freshmen are housed with one or two roommates. Despite the luxury of privacy, that is not altogether a bad thing: It can help you to make a new friend quickly and give you a dinner companion, especially important during those awkward first days away from home. Are you compulsively neat or cheerfully untidy? Does cigarette smoke make you wheeze and choke? Are you allergic to any animals? Make these facts known early, when they may have some bearing on the selection of your roommate.

If you find out the name of your roommate in advance, it is a good idea to contact him or her and either chat for a while on the phone or arrange a meeting if distance is not too great a problem. Discuss important likes and dislikes before moving in; it may avoid quarrels and unpleasantness later on. And if you discover that you really are incompatible, there may still be time to switch roommates with no hard feelings on either side.

Getting Along with a Roommate

Think for a moment about living with a brother or sister and all the problems—and occasional pleasures—of communal living, and it will give you some clues as to how to establish a good relationship with your college roommate.

Always respect the other person's privacy. Never snoop through drawers, books, closets, or personal possessions. Don't borrow books, records, clothing, or sports equipment without getting a clear go-ahead signal first. Don't read letters or other papers left lying around.

Be considerate. If you share a telephone, limit the number of calls that you make and the length of each one. Keep the noise level down to a minimum, especially at night, when your roommate may be trying to sleep or study, and in the early morning. Keep your personal possessions neat and orderly, not scattered randomly about the room.

Be Helpful. Are you a math whiz? Budding linguist? History buff? Maybe you can offer help to a roommate with his or her schoolwork if it doesn't interfere with your own. You will find that teaching is an excellent way of learning, and you may form a strong and long-lasting relationship in the process. If there is a phone call when your roommate is out or someone stops by to visit him or her, be sure to take an accurate message. Offer to bring food from the dining hall if your roommate is sick. All of these little things will help your relationship progress smoothly.

Exercising Caution

While you want to do everything in your power to establish a friendly and open relationship with your roommate, you also need to exercise a little discretion. Living with someone can mean that you develop a tight and exclusive bond that shuts out everyone else. You may make one good friend but also earn the reputation of being clannish and a snob. Try to broaden your horizons and make friends with a number of people.

You may also find yourself tempted to reveal everything to a roommate. Late-night talk sessions are spent baring intimate secrets and exchanging confidences. Like any friendship, this one needs to grow slowly. Remember that you will have to live with this person for the better part of a year. You may feel uncomfortable with things revealed too early, especially if it turns out that you do not become best friends with the person.

Better to use some restraint, at least at first, and pour out your heart to your diary, or to a best friend in a long, newsy letter.

Roommate Woes

Say you've tried everything—consideration, respect, openness, and warmth—but to no avail. You and your roommate simply cannot get along and can barely avoid snarling in each other's company. What should you do? Leave all the windows wide open when your roommate is a Southern boy shivering through his first New England winter? Hide your roommate's lab notes the night before the big biology test? In short, make every effort to show your displeasure and to be as mean, thoughtless, and spiteful as the law will reasonably allow?

The answer is a big, resounding *NO!* While such infantile

behavior may (and note, this is only *may*) make you feel a bit better for about fifteen minutes, it will not get you far in the long run. Think for a moment if the tables were turned and your roommate started pulling similar juvenile stunts on you. There is a lesson to be learned here, and you might as well learn it now. It is quite possible for two people who don't like each other to live together and still behave in a civilized and decent manner to each other. If everyone learned to do that, the world would certainly be a better place in which to live. Your life at school will be much easier and simpler if you are willing to accept this rule. Be as pleasant as you can under the circumstances. You don't have to lie and express affection and warmth when you feel none; no one expects you to buy flowers and other gifts for a roommate whom you really can't stand. But you should maintain a certain code of behavior and not let your ill will dominate the situation. Continue to take messages, exchange greetings, and the like. Don't waste your time and effort on antagonizing the other person. Instead, focus on finding a new and more agreeable living situation.

Your Home Away from Home

Another good reason to contact your new roommate in advance is to discuss room decor and furnishings. Most dormitories provide only the basics—bed, dresser, desk, and chair. After that, it's up to you. You and your roommate can talk about preferences and tastes, as well as ways of making the place more comfortable and homey. Maybe you can bring the old rug Mom's been storing in the attic, while your roommate agrees to bring curtains. There is no need for two stereo systems in one room, is there? One of you can save the expense and the trouble, and with luck your tastes are similar enough that you can share record albums. Both of you will need good desk lamps for late-night studying and typewriters for your papers. Think also about wastebaskets, alarm clocks, posters, plants, and cheerful bedspreads. Remember that you will be taking care of your own laundry, so be sure to have plenty of extra sheets and towels for those hectic exam weeks when you won't have time for washer and dryer. You also may want to take or buy a bookcase, but bricks and boards are an easy—and inexpensive—alternative. Don't neglect thrift shops and Salvation Army stores in your college or university area; you may be able to find an Art Deco velvet armchair for curling up with your books and a mug of coffee or an ornate standing lamp to go beside your bed or desk.

Living Off Campus

Some colleges allow and even encourage their students to live off campus, in houses or apartments. This option may sound very grownup and appealing—a place of your own—but you should think carefully before you choose it, particularly during the first year of school.

Remember that once on your own you will be responsible for all kinds of domestic chores. You will be shopping for food, cooking, doing the dishes, emptying the trash, and you may find it taxing when added to your academic responsibilities and your desire for an active social life. There will also be household bills to deal with, in addition to getting along with one and usually more housemates. You would no doubt learn a lot from such an experience, but it may be too much to handle in your college days. You should also keep in mind that living on your own may cut you off from certain aspects of campus life. No longer will you be eating communally with other students, which removes you from an important means of socializing; and if your house or apartment is any distance from the campus, you may discover that your desire to head over for a movie or a lecture is considerably decreased.

Making Friends and Socializing

After all the preparation and worries, you're finally there.

You've said good-bye to Mom and Dad, walked them to the car, and promised that you'll eat right, not stay out too late, and write to them once in a while. You head back to the dorm, where your two spanking new suitcases are waiting to be unpacked, and as you look around the bare room, you realize that you are alone in a strange place and don't know a single, solitary soul . . .

Don't panic! Everyone experiences the *angst* peculiar to a new place at one time or another, and although you may not know anyone yet, that won't last long, especially if you make just a slight effort to meet new friends with whom you can share these golden college days. Remember, there are lots of lonely freshmen out there at the very moment that you sit moping in your room, so what are you waiting for?

Be a Joiner

Everyone likes someone who likes things and takes an active part in what's going on. College life is known for its abundance of clubs, both social and academic, and you should make every effort to be part of your new world. Think about glee club or choir, French or Latin, lacrosse or drama or swimming. You will find a number of potential new friends who share your interest and enthusiasm.

Be a Doer

Especially in this transitional period, you must make the effort to meet others. Don't think it's forward to chat with someone sitting alone in the dining hall or in the dorm lounge. Tell yourself that you will attend a certain number of social events, such as dorm parties, lectures, readings, and films, in the interest of broadening your base of college friends.

Be a Starter

Why not be the one in your Intro Chem lab to suggest the

formation of a study group? Or the one on your dorm corridor to ask the others in for a study break of coffee and doughnuts? It is nice to have the reputation of being outgoing and friendly, and you will find it helps you to feel more comfortable and familiar in your new environment.

First Impressions

Now that you're at school and on your own, away from your family and childhood friends, you must realize that you will be meeting people from many kinds of upbringings and backgrounds. Some will be familiar to you; others will not. That is certainly no cause for alarm: It is a natural part of gaining experience in the world and becoming sophisticated. But you also want to put your best foot forward in new situations and have people walk away from their first encounter with you wanting to know you better.

You may find yourself with new groups of people quite often, and you certainly don't want them to find you lacking in the social graces. You must keep in mind all those rules that Mom drilled into you. Your napkin should be folded on your lap during a meal, and your feet planted firmly on the ground. No elbows on the table, eating with your fingers, or chewing with your mouth open. Take small bites, chew your food well. When drinking coffee or soup, remember that it is impolite to slurp. If you are confronted with an array of silverware at your place and don't know which fork to use for what course, don't panic; just progress from the outside to the inside and you'll be fine.

The early impression that you make may turn into a reputation—good or bad—that stays with you, so be sure that yours is a glowing one.

Your Academic Life

The main reason that you have come to college is to study and to learn. The work that will be expected of you as a college or university student is of a different caliber than that to which you have been accustomed. Both your classes and your assignments are likely to be more challenging and more rewarding than those of your high school days.

Bear in mind, however, that you will have to work harder to keep pace with the work load. In high school you may have had weekly quizzes in algebra or trig or Spanish to keep you on top of your work. You were probably given daily and weekly assignments, which were reviewed by your teacher and graded. You probably had the chance to participate in classes and could comment and question freely. All of that, along with the final exam, was part of your final grade in the course.

Now that you are in college, you may find that things are a bit different. Your classes will be large lectures with little, if any, opportunity for you to make your presence and personality felt. Rather than weekly assignments, you will have one or two major papers or exams. A good deal more independence is necessary for you to function, and you may have to learn to turn that to your advantage.

Developing Good Study Habits

Too many freshmen think that they can coast through the first weeks of the semester without doing any work or even opening a book. Instead, they plan to save all of their studying for two or three nights before the big exam. Don't you be one of those! Ten cups of coffee and chewing your nails down to the quick cannot substitute for a semester's disciplined and cumulative preparation. Learn to spend some time studying every single day. Go over your verb tenses for an hour each night. Do your reading for a literature class on a chapter-a-day basis. At the end of the week review your notebooks with a classmate, going over the lecture material and clarifying any misunderstandings with the professor or teaching assistant assigned to your section of the class. Then when exam time rolls around you can step up your routine, but only slightly. You won't have sleepless nights, for you will have been preparing steadily, all semester long. And you will probably receive very good grades as well.

Keep track of the assignments given out in all of your courses. If three papers fall due in one week, be sure to begin at least one of them a solid month in advance. Making yourself a timetable is a good way to keep your schoolwork flowing smoothly.

Also unlike high school, your classes will seldom be monitored, and there may be no one taking attendance. Don't let that encourage you to skip classes in favor of sleeping late or chatting with cronies over lunch. Attending classes regularly is the way to stay on top of the work load and not let it get on top of you.

Learn with a Friend

Study pals are a proven and effective way to aid the learning process. Team up with a friend in your class and make a regular practice of going over the material and testing each other on it. Teaching something to someone else is an excellent way to make sure that you fully comprehend it yourself. But in your efforts to be a good friend, don't let yourself get involved in anything unethical, such as writing a paper for someone or borrowing ideas without giving credit. Communal studying and cheating are not the same thing at all, so be very clear on the difference.

Your Professors

In college, your relationship to your professors is apt to be much less personal than it was in high school. The size of lectures and the use of teaching assistants can mean that you spend an entire semester in a class without your professor ever learning your name. If that bothers you, make the effort to seek out your professors after class or during their office hours. Don't be intimidated by their titles and degrees; they are there to teach you, and you are there to learn.

If you find that you are having trouble in a class, try seeking out the teacher directly instead of cutting class and hoping you can avoid the problem. Perhaps he or she can suggest a way to help. Extra work, outside reading, additional assignments, or even a tutoring session may help to clarify matters for you.

A technical point: A professor who has a doctorate should be addressed as Dr. or Professor. Assistant and associate professors with PhDs may be called Dr. as well. Otherwise, Mr., Mrs., Miss, or Ms. will suffice. Never call a teacher by a first name unless specifically invited to do so.

Attending classes well attired is a sign of respect for both the school and the teacher. Don't smoke or eat unless it is clearly permitted, and be sure you do so discreetly: no noisy crunching on apples or using the floor as an ashtray. Drink your morning coffee or afternoon tea *quietly*, and deposit all refuse in the wastebasket after class.

Students often become very close to a particular teacher. That can be a wonderful and rewarding experience and can enrich your life immeasurably. But be wary of any teacher who puts undue pressure on you. It is unethical for professors to conduct affairs with students, and anyone who does so is seriously compromising himself. Gracefully decline future invitations and ignore it unless the pressure continues. In that case, it may become harassment, and you may have to seek help from school authorities.

It is also common for college-age boys and girls to develop crushes on their professors. That is perfectly natural; they are people you look up to and admire. But don't confuse an infatuation of this kind with the possibility of a real romantic involvement. It is not appropriate for teachers and students to be involved in such a way. Fantasize all you like, but do not ask a teacher for a date if you have a crush on him or her. Avoid the rejection and possible embarrassment that will come of such behavior. Keep teachers as friends, but always maintain a slight distance.

The New Morality

As was mentioned before, the days of strictly single-sex living and parietals are over in many schools throughout the country. It is not at all uncommon for young men and women to share a bathroom or live on the same corridor. For many freshmen, this is the first time that parental rules and regulations have given way to a new and sometimes exhilarating sense of freedom. But that freedom can be a little dizzying, too, and make many teens anxious, especially those who are new to the college scene.

When you were living at home, you could pretty much depend on your parents to lay down ground rules for you to follow. You had to be home by a certain hour, and chances are that overnight guests of the opposite sex didn't share your room. But now that you are away from home you may find yourself in an environment where anything goes. It will be up to you to decide what you want to do and to stick by that choice.

Despite the new permissiveness, decisions about sexual intimacy are still very personal and should be made by you alone. The best advice anyone can give you is to follow the dictates of your heart and mind and ignore the advice and pressure of friends. Any date, boyfriend or girlfriend, who cannot respect your feelings is someone whose company you probably can do without.

If, on the other hand, you find that you are indeed ready for an intimate relationship, that is your own business, not that of your friends. But make sure you are aware of the potential risks and dangers. Be informed, and be prepared.

You may also find that many students are very casual about the use of liquor and drugs. Parties where liquor is served will be more and more frequent, and many students will use illegal drugs. You need to be careful about both, but especially the latter. Pot and hash may be taken for granted by the student body, but they aren't by the law. Don't forget for one moment that such drugs are illegal and use of them could be grounds for your expulsion from school.

Liquor, although legal if you are of age, should be used in moderation. Hangovers will improve neither your school work nor your social life, and no one invites a sloppy or rowdy drunk back again.

Learn to hold your liquor. Never drink on an empty stomach, and sip drinks slowly rather than gulping them down. Don't mix different kinds of liquor. You will enjoy liquor more if you learn to savor and appreciate it. Fine wines and champagnes, good whiskies, and cordials all have their own special flavors, which are best enjoyed in small quantities.

The Social Whirl

After the initial uncertainty and shyness wear off, many teenagers find that their college days are unparalleled in the excitement and flurry of social activity. Parties and dates, late-night pizzas and beers, clubs and fraternities, and just sitting around listening to the stereo with your roommate—these can be some of the most fun-filled times of your life.

You *should* enjoy yourself at school. The social and interpersonal skills that you develop there will last you a lifetime. But at the same time, don't forget the real reason that you came to school—to get an education. There is no reason that you shouldn't get the very best education possible.

That means learning to compromise. You will learn to give and take, indulge and deny, to weigh long-term satisfactions against short-term pleasures. You will have to monitor yourself; no one is looking over your shoulder anymore. In short, you will be using this time to grow up.

You will learn how and when to study and to develop routines that are uniquely yours. Perhaps you will devote yourself to the books five nights a week and party on the weekends. Or you may find that you like to work late at night, when most people are asleep and the distractions are few. Or maybe you hit the sack early and get up with the birds to get your assignments done. Maybe you'll do a French marathon one night, anthropology the next, and so on; or maybe you'll give all your courses an hour a night. The choice is really yours, and as long as the results are good, it doesn't matter how you decide to structure your time.

This will be a time of many new decisions and an evaluation of your priorities. You are striving for balance, something that you can use all of your adult days. Remember that all work and no play . . . Four years of college without a single prom, football game, all-night party just wouldn't be college somehow. You need pleasure, just as you need discipline, and you need to find a way to give yourself both.

CHAPTER VIII

On the Go: Tips for Traveling

As a child, the extent of your travel experience was probably limited to summer camps and trips with your family. But as a budding adult, you will be traveling more and more with your friends on your own. Weekends are spent at colleges and universities, visiting another state, exploring a new city or town, or just relaxing in some idyllic rural setting.

Traveling can be a wonderful and enriching experience, opening your heart and mind to new sights and sounds, whole other vistas. But traveling well, with the maximum of pleasure and the minimum of discomfort, is something that is learned, and sometimes through trial and error. This chapter will alert you to some of the pitfalls of traveling and help you avoid them so that all your journeys will be memorable for the right reasons.

Plan in Advance

When you are about to embark upon a trip, be it a weekend jaunt or a two-month voyage, you want to be well prepared for it. That may take careful research and planning; good trips are made, they don't just happen. Too many things can go wrong for you to leave them to chance, or the last minute. Learn to plan early, and enjoy your trips for years to come.

How Will You Travel?

First of all, how are you going to reach your destination? Let's consider some of the most common modes of travel today.

Automobile. Plan your route with the aid of maps and guidebooks. If you're driving with friends, decide how you want to split up the driving and the expenses, so that each person knows what his or her share is to be. Pooling funds is often a good idea, with everyone pitching in for gasoline, tolls, and so on. Be sure the car has been inspected by a competent professional, particularly if you are going any distance. Maps are essential, as are a spare tire, a jack, and a flashlight. Take a blanket in cool weather, and plenty of snacks, including a thermos of hot coffee to see you through.

Bus. Obtain a current schedule. Find out by calling the bus station if you need to reserve a seat in advance or can safely leave it until the day of departure. Do you need to arrive early if the seating is first come first served? Take along plenty to eat; bus station food is terrible, and it's not likely the driver will stop at your favorite fast-food restaurant along the way. For bus travel, as well as plane and train, head phones for your radio can make your travel time speed by without bothering your neighbors.

Trains. Check schedules, seating availability, and suggested time of arrival at the station. Trains usually have dining cars, so you probably need not take food. But do take books, magazines, a deck of cards, and crossword puzzles to keep you amused and occupied during the trip. Train seats almost always have pull-out trays for your convenience. Remember that in all traveling holiday and weekend departures are usually more crowded. Reserve seats for those times well in advance, and get there early enough to claim them.

Airplane. Tickets are purchased in advance, except for some short shuttle flights, charters, or stand-bys. Call the airport and double-check the departure time before leaving home; planes are often delayed and can easily be hours behind schedule. Give yourself plenty of time to get to the airport without rushing; it is a good idea to arrive early, especially for overseas flights. Take along some chewing gum to reduce ear discomfort when taking off and landing. If you're having someone meet you at the airport, give him or her the flight number, airline, and scheduled arrival time, so that they too can call and check. Your baggage should have clearly marked identification on it. Take along a sweater or a light jacket; planes can be quite chilly, no matter what the season.

Packing

You want to be as comfortable as possible on your trip, and that means taking along only things that you will really need and use. Unless you are backpacking through the woods, most items are readily available for purchase, of course. But buying a beach hat in a resort town is apt to be more expensive than if you had shopped for it at home. And who wants to waste precious travel time shopping for a sweater, mittens, or a bathing suit because they have failed to pack properly?

Weather

Often a bit of research is in order to find out what kind of weather can be expected, but despite your foresight the weather cannot be predicted with one hundred percent certainty. Dressing in layers is a good way to be prepared for almost anything. Any combination of jacket, shirt, sweater, and the like can be worn together or in a variety of combinations, depending on the temperature. This is an especially good idea for the spring and fall, which often bring variable weather conditions. In winter, unless you are traveling south, you will need your warmest coat, good boots, hat, scarf, gloves, and perhaps an umbrella. If you plan to be outdoors a great deal, go equipped with lip balm and body lotions, as well as glasses to protect against snow glare. The "climate" of your room can also be unpredictable, so take warm pajamas; and a robe is always an excellent idea no matter what the season.

In the warm months you will want a swimsuit or two, sun hat, glasses, comfortable shoes, and something to wear after swimming to protect against sun and wind. Sunburn can ruin a good time, so take care to cover up.

Remember, too, that even summer can have cool nights and that air conditioning can lower the temperature indoors. Take along a light sweater or jacket as well as a long-sleeved shirt or blouse, even in June, July, and August.

Consider Your Plans

If your trip involves a lot of sightseeing or car travel, pack comfortable shoes and clothes that don't inhibit or restrict movement. Take along knits and other wrinkle-free fabrics so that you can look fresh and neat without having to press your clothes. If your trip involves a formal occasion such as a wedding or dance, you might think of investing in a garment bag that can be hung in a car, bus, or plane to protect your fancy clothes. Most hotels will provide an iron for a nominal charge.

Should your trip involve backpacking or camping out, you are best off in a sporting goods store or department. You will want very specific kinds of clothing and equipment, and your needs can best be met by a specialist.

Pack Light

Especially if you intend to be moving around frequently or carrying your bags yourself, opt for clothes that can mix and match: three blouses or shirts that go with all your pants, shoes that go with everything, one jacket to top it all off. You can thus maximize the use of any single garment and cut down on excess. Remember, too, that a small box of laundry detergent and a traveling clothesline (purchased in a pharmacy, notions, or department store) can save you from carrying too many changes of clothing. It's nice to feel relatively unencumbered on a trip; sometimes you can even avoid the wait at the baggage claim area of an airport if you confine yourself to two pieces of carry-on luggage that can be stowed above or below your seat. And you do want to save some room for souvenirs of the trip!

To sum up, here is a quick travel checklist. Feel free to add to it or make one of your own.

1. Extra dimes for emergency calls.
2. Up-to-date address and phone book (with names and numbers of those you may visit!)
3. Aspirin
4. Gum or throat lozenges, cough drops, mints
5. Medication for motion sickness
6. In summer months: tanning lotion, moisturizer, sunglasses, hat, antihistamine (allergies or hayfever can ruin your summer fun), witch hazel or calamine lotion for insect bites, and repellent to ward them off
7. In winter months: hat or ear muffs, umbrella, waterproof boots, extra gloves, scarf, warm socks, pajamas, lip balm, body lotion
8. Comfortable and supportive shoes, sneakers
9. Sweater or jacket
10. Camera, film, flash bulbs
11. Stamps for postcards

Traveling With Friends

Traveling with friends is an excellent idea, especially if you are new to the travel scene. It gives you an automatic companion for sightseeing, meals, beaches—whatever, and it is fun to share your perceptions of a new place with someone else. But you should also be aware that traveling with another person means a certain amount of compromise.

Talk about your plans before you go. Discuss how you want to handle matters such as money and driving. Are you and your friend on the same kind of budget? Is it four-star hotels or inexpensive bed-and-breakfast places? Make sure that you have talked about all this in advance of your trip.

Prepare a list of your preferences: the must-sees, the things you could possibly sacrifice, and the things in which you have no interest at all. Have your friend or friends do the same, and see if the lists coordinate. If they do, great, but if they don't, that's OK too. Going with a friend doesn't mean that you must spend every moment of your time together. You should feel free to laze around at the beach all morning, working on your tan and listening to the ocean, while your friend is off at a naval museum, a botanical garden, or fast asleep in bed. Later you can meet for lunch and talk about how you spent the morning.

If you are going to share a room, remember to be polite and respect the other person's privacy. Let him or her select the bed first, and make a note of when your friend prefers to use the bathroom. Use your common sense and consideration: Don't wake people late at night or early in the morning, or make excessive noise. If you use room service or make long-distance phone calls, be sure to pay for them when the time comes.

If you are traveling in a group larger than two or three, you may find that you have to compromise a bit more. No sleeping in until noon while everyone waits for you in the lobby, impatient and angry. You have to get a sense of the group's energy and direction and make an effort to go along with it. Of course, you may on occasion opt to spend some time alone; that's fine as long as it doesn't become a habit. If you are a constant loner, your friends may feel insulted and wonder why you agreed to the trip if you don't enjoy their company.

Girls and Boys Together

Sometimes you may be thrown together with people of the opposite sex on a group trip. It may be that girls and boys are expected to share sleeping facilities and bathrooms. If this happens to you, you can handle the situation with grace and maturity. Make a schedule for the bathroom, and don't abuse it. Don't play practical jokes on anyone such as not respecting privacy and modesty. Wear a robe when in the room undressed, and consider this part of your training for the adult world.

Group Travel

When you go on a trip with your class at school, a church

group, a glee club, or a sports team, you are a representative of that group or institution and your behavior reflects upon it. You want to make a good impression and have people welcome you—and your group—back again.

When you are in your hotel or motel room, be considerate of other guests. Keep your radio and television set playing at a reasonable volume. Feel free to have fun with other members of your group, but don't let that fun get out of hand or excessively rowdy. No television at full blast with the door open wide waiting for your buddies—and the management—to come in!

Use your room, but don't abuse it. Soap, towels, glasses, and ashtrays are there for your comfort while you are on the premises, not as souvenirs for your friends at home. Don't destroy or damage any property, and do leave the room in a respectable fashion—trash in the wastebaskets, blankets and pillows on the beds. Of course, this is one visit where you don't have to make your bed in the morning.

When you are in public, try to restrain your high spirits a bit. You may have noticed that groups of teenagers tend to get somewhat noisy. Everyone wants to be the center of attention and is vying for the position of group leader. Under those circumstances, it is all too easy to become a bit rambunctious. But resist that impulse to go tearing down the main street of a strange town or city at breakneck speed, or to toss water balloons out of your hotel windows at innocent passersby. Such behavior will make an impression, but not the one that you want to leave behind.

When traveling in a group, you should obey your teacher or whoever is responsible for you. If you are told to be in by a certain hour, abide by that decision. Don't go to places that have been deemed off-limits, or deliberately flout rules. You will only make things more difficult for the person in charge and, ultimately, for yourself.

Don't forget the purpose of the trip. Are you with the school band? Then don't skip rehearsal. As part of a social studies class? Be sure you attend the planned outings. When traveling on your own you can plan your itinerary, but until then you should be on your best behavior. If you are branded a trouble-maker on this trip, the next time you may not be asked along.

Do remember that class trips and the like are an excellent way to socialize and get to know a number of different people. You may have your own crowd at school, but make an effort to talk with at least one person you don't know very well. You are in a new place to expand and broaden your horizons, socially as well as intellectually, so take advantage of the opportunity.

Foreign Soil

Many people wait until their twenties or even early thirties before they have a chance to travel to a foreign country. But with airplane travel becoming more affordable all the time, teens abroad are quite a common phenomenon these days. You may be planning a graduation trip or a summer excursion. Whatever it is, you want to have a great time, and that means planning ahead.

Know Your Destination

Whether you visit one new country or ten, you should have at least rudimentary knowledge about the place. Your trip will be much more meaningful if you have some background on history, customs, and language. Read guidebooks carefully and choose sites that you want to see. You can borrow books from the library, but it is a good idea, especially on a first trip, to own one if not two guidebooks. The same is true for street maps that indicate major sites and clearly marked pedestrian routes. If you can, take a crash course in the language before your departure, or brush up on a language that you have studied in school. It will help you get around and give you a sense of the place. If you can, make a rough itinerary, so that you'll have some idea of how long you want to spend in each stop-off point of your journey.

Be Prepared

Nothing is worse than being stranded in a foreign country without the proper clothing, equipment, or supplies. Make sure you know about the weather and the climate before you leave, and pack accordingly. You can call or write to the U.S. tourist office of many countries for up-to-date information about what to wear and to take with you. Be sure to pack any medications that you might need, as well as cosmetics or toiletries that might be difficult to find abroad.

When in Rome . . .

In a foreign country it is advisable to adhere as much as possible to the prevailing customs and codes of behavior. Don't offend people if you don't have to. Never deride or ridicule a form of behavior that you don't understand; instead, try to analyze it in your mind to discover what it might mean or what might be its origin.

Allow for differences in dress and manners. In some countries men kiss on both cheeks in greeting; in others, white is the color of mourning. In some situations, you can wear a bathing suit to the dinner table; in others, formal attire is required. You should know which is which by observing and then follow the customs.

Religious institutions often have their own standards of modesty, to which you should conform. If, for example, you visit medieval churches on a Spanish pilgrimage route, you should not wear short shorts or a halter top.

In some countries salad is served after the main course, and dessert consists of fruit and cheese. Enjoy the differences in cuisine rather than imposing your own customs. Who knows, maybe you'll learn to love calves' brains or raw fish! That's what travel is all about.

You can learn a lot about a people's values if you observe their ways carefully. Be a watcher: Look for the disparities in dress, clothing, types of work, religious ceremonies, holidays, and you'll begin to get a sense of what other lives are really like. You might want to keep a travel diary and record your observations so that you can think about them when you are back home.

Being Careful

You may not realize it at first, but you are more vulnerable in a strange country than on your own turf. Everything about this new place is different and unfamiliar to you: the streets, food, customs, climate, scenery, and often language. This newness and strangeness can be exhilarating, even intoxicating. It is part of the enchantment that a foreign place can weave around us. But you should be aware that you are in a different environment and take a few simple precautions when traveling alone or with friends.

Your Possessions. Don't take things of extreme sentimental or material value unless you really need them. Expensive jewelry, fragile clothing, irreplaceable mementos aren't necessary to your enjoyment. In the flurry of packing and unpacking, strange hotel rooms and train compartments, it is all too easy to leave something precious behind. Also, recognize that crime does exist, and it would be a great pity to have valuable or loved items stolen while traveling. So be smart and leave your treasures safe at home.

Of course, you will have with you some important and valuable things, such as passports and money, camera, and binoculars. Travelers checks are a wise idea, but remember to store their identification numbers *separate* from the checks. In that way, if they are lost or stolen it is possible to have them replaced without being liable yourself. Don't leave valuables unattended in your room. If you won't be needing them, have them securely locked up at the front desk, a service that most hotels are glad to provide. Always lock your door when in your room for the night, as well as when you leave it for the day. Put your belongings away neatly rather than strewing them carelessly about the room; it will be much easier to keep track of them that way.

Keep track of your possessions while out sightseeing, too: Look for bags, cases, and clothing with inside zippers, secure handles, and deep pockets. There are also special cases to be worn around your waist to conceal money and passport rather than leaving them potentially exposed in a pocket or handbag.

Street Smarts. Remember that you are not at home, and exercise care when out and about on the streets of a strange country. Don't be afraid to ask people for directions and assistance, but always be alert and use your own good judgment about them. Don't get into cars with people you don't know or have just met, and *never* hitchhike—that is just asking for trouble!

Never go with a new acquaintance down a dark or poorly lit street. Stay where it's crowded at night; people usually represent some measure of safety. Your vacation should not be spent in fear and anxiety, but you do want to learn to look out for yourself now, so that it will simply become one of your good habits—like brushing your teeth, or fastening a safety belt.

When out alone at night, indulge yourself and take a taxi back to your hotel rather than walking unescorted. Don't venture into unfamiliar neighborhoods after dark; save your exploring for daylight hours. If you find that you are lost, don't panic. Try to find a policeman, a uniformed official, or even a shopkeeper to ask for directions.

Your Health. Increased activity, jet lag, late nights, extremes of heat or cold can weaken your resistance while traveling. You may find that the food or water in a foreign country disagrees with you, particularly in hot climates. It is advisable to avoid tap water unless it has been boiled first to kill any impurities. Opt instead for bottled water, juice, or soft drinks. In extremely hot climates meat, poultry, and fish tend to spoil more quickly and could give you food poisoning. Eat lighter meals, with an emphasis on cooked fruits and vegetables, grains and other starches. Enjoy spicy foreign delicacies, too, but in moderation: The wonderful curry you wolf down at dinner could keep you up with heartburn later on.

The Folks Back Home

As a teen who travels, you should consider yourself lucky to have the chance to see something of the world at such an early stage. Wouldn't you like to share a little of that luck with those you love back home?

Picture postcards. Even if you hate writing, the message can be short and sweet, and they're a quick and easy way to let people know you're thinking of them.

Letters. On longer trips you should sit down and make the effort to write home to your parents and other close relatives and friends. Share the wonders that you've seen with them, and all the new and exciting things you've been experiencing. If you're feeling lonely or homesick or just having an awful time (which does, alas, happen!), writing is a good way to get it off your chest and to feel closer to those you've left behind.

Phone calls. Make long-distance calls brief, because they are very costly. But Mom and Dad will be thrilled to hear your voice and to know that you've arrived safely so they can stop worrying about you.

Gifts. You certainly don't have to spend a fortune, but carrying back small mementos is a lovely way of telling the people you care about that you've missed them. Choose small, easily packed items, things that are not likely to break. Try to select gifts that capture something of the local color or spirit, not something that could just as easily be purchased back home.

Photographs. There is no better way to share where you've been and what you've seen than through the magic eye of a camera. Load up on film and flash bulbs, and just snap away!

CHAPTER IX

Engagement and Marriage

You may be too young to be getting married yourself, but you will undoubtedly be in the position of observing friends who are becoming engaged and making wedding plans. And certainly it is a subject that will be on your mind, if not for the present, then for some time in the future.

Most of us look forward with anticipation to the day when we can make that special promise to someone we love and pledge our loyalty and commitment in the universally accepted ceremony of marriage. This chapter is designed to deal with some of the social rituals that accompany this holy rite and to keep you up-to-date about wedding procedures, whether you are an observer or a prospective participant. There is also a brief final section on living together, an increasingly common phenomenon among young people, and how to deal with the social implications and reverberations of that life-style.

Popping the Question—For Him

In Hollywood movies everything always goes perfectly. The lovers move effortlessly into each other's arms, the music swells to a crescendo, and no words are needed to express their overwhelming, passionate, and eternal love. But for the rest of us earthly mortals, a bit of help is sometimes needed in trying to articulate those feelings.

A proposal of marriage to a girl shouldn't come as a bolt from the blue to her. You should give her clues as to your feelings for her and be aware of the messages, verbal or not, that she is sending you. Usually, she will get the idea that you feel a special way about her, and hopefully she will return the sentiment. But as liberated as today's young woman may be, she probably won't ask you to marry her, so you'll have to be the one to do it.

No one can tell you what to say or how to say it; love is a unique and personal experience for each of us. But here are a few hints about when to ask for her hand and when it would be better to keep quiet.

Good Moments

1. Sitting together in front of a glowing fire, with her head on your shoulder and your arm snugly around her waist.
2. Splashing through a summer rainstorm together, holding hands and laughing about nothing.
3. After she's just said, "I love you."
4. When she calls long distance for no reason except to say that she misses you.
5. After she's sent *you* flowers!
6. When she tells you that she likes you even better than chocolate.
7. If she tells you how much she loves your family.

Bad Moments

1. After she's had a rotten day, *and* you've kept her waiting in the rain for an hour.
2. When you notice that she never laughs at your jokes anymore.
   If she's lost the ring/pin/necklace/bracelet you gave her for her birthday and *you're* the one who notices.
4. When she tells you it might be best if you both started to see other people.
5. After she gives you a good-night handshake instead of a kiss.

Getting Engaged

Now that you've both decided that you care for each other and want to seal the relationship for ever and always, you must tell your parents—both sets—of your decision. Often, your folks will have a good idea that Jack, George, Connie, or Peg is a pretty special person in your life, and they may even be expecting the announcement of a son or daughter-in-law being added to the family. Drop hints if you can, and *let* them suspect. Don't keep your romance a total secret; unwelcome reactions can arise from shock or surprise. You might even say things like, "If Kate and I were to get married . . ." or, "We've been thinking about getting more serious," to clue them in early.

You might want to have your intended with you when you deliver the news. It can often make things a bit easier for you, and it is certainly appropriate. While it is no longer necessary for a young man to ask for a girl's hand in marriage, you will probably endear yourself to her father if you do.

In-Laws

If your two families do not already know each other, this is the right time to remedy that situation. Plan a get-together—dinner or lunch at a restaurant removes the burden of entertaining—so that the parents can meet in a leisurely way in the presence of their soon-to-be-wed children. You might also invite any sisters and brothers or another close family member such as a grandmother or grandfather. Of course you hope that everyone will like one another and get along, but you can help to make conversation easy and smooth between the two families. Since you and your bride or groom-to-be have the advantage of knowing all those present, it is up to you to set the ball rolling in conversation. Be sure to direct questions and remarks to various members of the group, rather than exclusively to one or two. Think ahead of interests that are shared and subtly inject them into the conversation. For instance, if both your father and your fiancée's are sailing buffs, or follow the stock market closely, ask them strategic questions and then let them take it on their own. In-law friction can be a source of trouble to a newly married couple, so the better your new in-laws like your parents, the easier your married life will be.

Length of Engagement

Many people are concerned about the proper length of an engagement. There is really no right answer. People used to allow months or even years between the announcement and the wedding. Short engagements were frowned upon.

Nowadays couples can decide for themselves. If you or your fiancée are in school, you may want to postpone the wedding until after graduation. Also, a large wedding requires longer planning and hence a longer engagement.

The engagement period also allows both partners to "try on" the idea of marriage before entering upon it, and it enables the world to begin to see them as a permanently attached couple. But all that notwithstanding, you can still have a short engagement and not be thought of any the worse.

The Shower

The shower is a familiar and pleasant ritual for congratulating the bride. Generally it is made up of the girl's closest friends and female relatives. Men are traditionally excluded, and it is more like a ladies' lunch or tea than a coed party.

It is customary for a close friend or relative to be the hostess. Surprise showers are common, although the surprise element is by no means mandatory. Some girls prefer to have a hand in compiling the guest list, deciding on the food, and so on. And some people do not enjoy surprise parties of any kind; better find out before you make plans to throw one.

Showers are often structured around a theme, which gives the guests inspiration for their gifts. Following are some suggestions for theme showers.

Round-the-Clock Shower. Each guest is given an hour of the day and brings a present that is appropriate for use at that time. For example, the 8:00 A.M. gift might be a set of cheerful mugs or a lacquered breakfast tray; 9:00 P.M. might be a bottle of fine wine or some elegant glasses in which to serve it.

Color Shower. The bride may already have chosen a color scheme for certain rooms in her new house or apartment. Guests are told in advance and select their gifts according to her design scheme. If her new bedroom is to be melon, beige, and tan, think about sheets in those tones, a pretty ceramic reading lamp, or even framed prints in which those shades predominate.

Room Shower. Each guest is assigned a room in the couple's new home and brings a gift that can be used in it. One might buy placemats and matching napkins for the dining room, a shower curtain or fluffy rug for the bathroom, a crystal vase or ashtray for the living room.

Seasonal Shower. The guests are given one of the four seasons and select a gift that can be used at that time of year (of course, more than one guest will be bringing a gift for each season, but that's fine). Those who have "summer" might choose an attractive wicker picnic hamper or a glass pitcher for iced tea or lemonade; the "winter" guest might opt for a popcorn maker (wonderful on a cold winter night, right?) or a soft goosedown quilt. Be creative in your gift-giving: What about a sled, snorkeling equipment? Gifts can be amusing as well as practical.

The Stag Party

Stag parties used to be known for their male exclusivity, wild pranks, and "blue" entertainment. They were thrown to give the groom a last taste of freedom and wild oats before he accepted the bonds of matrimony.

Today, however, stag parties are considered by many people to be a bit sexist and old-fashioned. If you are interested in throwing one for a best buddy, better check with the bride first and get a sense of her feelings about the proposed bash. You don't want to create any more static to add to their wedding jitters. If she objects to the idea, you should drop it and plan instead for a less exclusive sort of party, with both male and female guests—who knows, it may even be more fun in the long run!

In General

Stag parties, showers, and engagement parties tend to be less strictly formal affairs than the wedding itself, and you need not fear that you are flouting convention if you plan them that way. You may wish to have your pre-wedding celebration in the daytime or the evening, home-cooked or catered, with many friends and acquaintances or only the closest few.

You might want to plan a traditional party, using some of the guidelines suggested later in this chapter, but many couples feel that with the preparations for the wedding already under way, a simpler kind of celebration is in order. Consider a dinner party at a favorite restaurant, or a brunch for some of your best friends. An engagement cocktail party can also avoid the headaches of an elaborate catered party. Serve champagne, of course, a selection of wines, and a few well-chosen snacks.

Gifts for Him and Her

At the shower people generally try to bring gifts that the couple can use together when they are married. Often these gifts are designed to help the young couple who are just starting out to furnish their nest and to make it more attractive and comfortable. Gifts at the stag party tend to be more comic in nature and often involve gags, jokes, or pranks. All of these options are certainly appropriate to the occasion, but why not be a little different? The shower, stag party, or engagement party may be the last social function where the bride and groom are not yet an established couple, so why not get them each something that they can use *alone* rather than as a pair? Not that I have anything against togetherness per se, but the joining of two individuals in marriage should mean ideally the creation of something *new*, and not the obliteration of what already exists.

Think about giving the bride scented bubble bath, hand cream, or talcum powder with a great big puff. Or some attractive article of clothing, such as a blouse, scarf, sweater, or gloves. Or a new book that she has been wanting to read. Think along the same lines for the groom: new clothing, records, books, sporting equipment—something that will be uniquely his. These kinds of gifts make rather special statements to the couple and can be deeply appreciated by those who receive them. Remember, good marriages are those that can accommodate two separate individuals; let your gift reflect this small celebration of individuality.

When You Are the Recipient

Engagement gifts should be accepted with graciousness and politeness. You should endeavor to appear delighted with the gift, even if you don't care for it or have received three just like it already. How could Aunt Alice know that you had been given two bathroom scales before hers arrived?

Gifts should be acknowledged by a hand-written thank-you note. Even if you are planning to return it to the store the very next day, that should not prevent you from making the correct gesture of appreciation.

Planning the Wedding

Planning a wedding can be one of the most exciting things you have ever done, but it can also be one of the most irritating and emotionally draining. You may find that you are quarreling so much with everyone—including your beloved—or feeling so worn out that you would rather elope and dispense with all the bother.

That is certainly one way of solving the problem, but it is not necessarily the best. A marriage ceremony is not only an important commitment made between two loving individuals; it also has a public and social function, which joins the couple together in the eyes of man as well as those of God. It is a beautiful and life-affirming ritual, and with planning and foresight it can be the memorable day that it should be. Don't let the complications bog you down; after all, most worthwhile things take some preparation and hard work.

When you have decided on an approximate number of guests to be invited to your wedding, make a timetable with a "wedding countdown." You do this by selecting the actual wedding day (give yourself a couple of alternatives, in case your pastor is busy or the banquet hall is already reserved) and counting backwards from it. How many weeks will it take to order, address, and mail invitations? Find the perfect dress? Engage a caterer? Your timetable should have marks for each step along the way, so that you know where you are supposed to be with the preparations at all times. If you have planned carefully and can stick to your schedule, you shouldn't have many last-minute foulups and headaches.

The Invitation

There are many ways to handle the wedding invitation. Some couples decide on a very intimate ceremony, confined to family members and a few close friends, and a big party afterwards. If that describes your plan, you might send out invitations to the reception but not the ceremony to all those people who will be invited to the latter.

On the other hand, if the guest list for the reception has grown too large, you can send some people invitations to the ceremony only.

Naturally, you must provide your prospective guests with a way of responding to your invitation. It is usual to include an RSVP card, with an engraved message such as: "I/We will /will not have the pleasure of attending your wedding . . .". You must also include a self-addressed, stamped envelope. Some people, however, expect the invitees to accept or decline with a hand-written note. If that is how you are handling your invitation list, be sure to provide the correct address so that the reply will reach you in time.

Invitations can be sent as a form of announcement as well, and if you do that, include all parts of the invitation. You may not expect the guests from Brazil or Japan to arrive, but you should nonetheless extend them the courtesy of receiving it in its entirety.

You will want to consult with a printer or engraver to select typeface and paper stock. Often, wedding invitations are done in an elegant script rather than block printing, which lends a formal and graceful note to the final printed product.

The Guest List

The guest list for your wedding is really a matter of personal choice and personal finances. Some people see the wedding as an extravaganza, an elaborate social occasion to which they want to invite almost everyone they know. Such a guest list will include family, friends, friends of friends, business acquaint-ances, and people who are really guests of the parents or other family members. The occasion generally involves a formal ceremony followed by a large party.

Other couples prefer the intimacy of a small family group with possible addition of a few close friends. And of course, many weddings are planned for groups that range anywhere between the two extremes.

If you start with an organized guest list, it will be easier to keep track of those who are actually coming to the wedding. Consult your parents and those of your fiancée for suggestions on choosing the guests. And of course you and your intended will have some ideas of your own that you will want to discuss together.

When you have finally arrived at some kind of list, print it neatly, or better still, type it. Avoid having tiny slips of paper all over the place. Prepare the list in alphabetical order. Include everyone who will actually receive an invitation (if you are separating ceremony from reception, make sure your list indicates that, too), and make columns marked *Yes* or *No* in which you can check off the names as the responses come in. That will give you an accurate record of who has been invited and who will be there. You might even want to note the date that the response was received. This list will be invaluable as your plans progress. You can use it for food and seating arrangements as well as for writing thank-you notes for the wedding presents, especially if you have included addresses.

Ceremonies Old and New

Traditional wedding ceremonies are religious. If you and your intended are of the same faith and share the same religious values and beliefs, you should consult the appropriate religious leader for advice and guidance. Depending upon the orthodoxy of the person whom you select, the ceremony may adhere to a definite format, or it may leave room for interpolation of more personal sentiments.

Many younger couples prefer to add words of their own choosing to a wedding service, because they feel that the liturgical language is no longer the most appropriate vehicle for the expression of their feelings. They may choose lines of verse or passages from the Bible or another meaningful text. They may even compose their own vows. If you want a less traditional ceremony, consult the person who will be performing it. If he or she cannot accede to your wishes for religious reasons, perhaps he can refer you to someone who will.

Sometimes the bride and groom are not of the same faith. Statistics show that this phenomenon is on the rise, and it can (although surely it need not) create some problems. Some religions permit intermarriage and their leaders will marry members of different faiths. Others will not and may refuse to perform the ceremony unless one member converts to that particular religion. You and your fiancée should openly and honestly discuss your religious beliefs and come to a mutually satisfying agreement about the type of ceremony you will have.

Another alternative is the civil ceremony, which is performed by a justice of the peace or other civil official. As long as the two people have a license, and meet the legal requirements for blood tests and age of consent, they can be legally wed by the state's representative, and their religious beliefs are of no consequence.

Location

You have many choices as to where to hold your wedding. Couples often select a church, cathedral, or temple for the ceremony and a private home, rented hall, or hotel banquet room for the reception. If you wish, however, you can have both the ceremony and the reception in one place, provided the minister, priest, or rabbi is willing to officiate outside the house of worship.

A wedding reception held in the home has the charm of intimacy and familiarity. The comfortable setting can make for an atmosphere that is both warm and appealing. And it can save you money. But there is also much preparation and hard work involved in handling the reception yourselves or with the sole aid of parents and a few friends. Many couples opt for a rented space, a hotel banquet room, a community center, or communal rooms in the church to eliminate this particular step from their wedding preparations.

Decorations and Food

Your decorations and choice of food will depend upon where you have decided to hold the wedding, as well as the time of year.

If you are having your wedding at home, you will want to start with a spotless house. Count on a few days before the affair to be scrubbing, buffing, polishing, and scouring for a spanking-fresh setting. Think about fresh flowers, candles, wreaths, festive tablecloths, napkins, and dishes. Many companies rent such paraphernalia; consult your local yellow pages.

If you intend to have a sit-down dinner, you may dispense with the formality of place cards, but by all means use the fanciest china, crystal, silverware, and linens that you can get your hands on. You may want to order centerpieces from a florist, or if the roses are blooming you can create your own. Candles will adorn any table, sideboard, buffet, or credenza, so let there be lights!

Many wedding receptions held at home, however, do not involve a formal meal. You can opt instead for a buffet, which is more casual and easier to plan and serve, or just drinks and hors d'oeuvres. I have heard of one couple who, at a June wedding reception, served nothing but fresh strawberries, mountains of whipped cream, and free-flowing champagne. It may have been limited fare, but it was certainly elegant and sophisticated!

Catered weddings cost more, but they may be easier on your strained nerves at this hectic time. It is not so hard to conceptualize a multicourse dinner if you know that someone else will be planning and serving it. Seating arrangements can vary. You may seat all of the guests at one large table if that is possible. But if the group has become too large, you will have to divide them up among several tables. Between six and twelve is a good number for these smaller tables. Formal name cards are not necessary at a wedding, and dispensing with them allows for an ease and congeniality of atmosphere. If you are planning on several tables, you might indicate to your guests on their invitations where they should seat themselves. It is customary to seat husbands and wives as well as boyfriends and girlfriends at the same table.

Catered affairs can range from a formal sit-down meal of several courses to buffet-style service where the guests help themselves or are served by members of the catering staff and then seat themselves at tables. The catered affair also can be confined to drinks—plenty of champagne, please!—and hors d'oeuvres. If you choose the latter, plan the reception between meal times and say "Cocktails will be served" on the invitation, so that your guest will not show up starved and expecting a five-course meal.

Music

Music is a traditional part of many, if not most, weddings. They are, after all, a time of joyous celebration, and what better way to celebrate than with the sweet strains of music?

You may want to have an organist play the traditional wedding march as you and your beloved walk down the aisle, or you may choose other appropriate music. Many couples want live music for the dancing that will follow the ceremony. If you engage professional musicians for your wedding, you should discuss in advance the kind of music to be played. It is often a good idea to have a wide range of musical genres: traditional, folk, romantic, contemporary and popular, jazz, rock, and disco, so that many tastes are represented. Some people will dance only to a waltz; others prefer the hustle or the Texas two-step, and you want everyone to join the dance.

The Icing on the Cake . . .

Finally on the subject of food, what would a wedding be without the wedding cake? Whether it is six tiers of perfectly iced angel food delight, complete with spun sugar swans and a miniature statuette of the happy couple, or a homemade sponge cake on a pretty paper lace doily, it is an integral part of any wedding, and you should be sure to include it to sweeten your own.

Dress

Traditionally, weddings have been considered very formal occasions. In our society it is customary to see the bride all in white and the groom in full formal dress, tuxedo or tails. Things have changed, however, and today wedding attire can be less formal yet still perfectly appropriate. Many modern young women and girls find it too costly to invest in a dress that they will wear only once and then give to a daughter, relative, or friend. They prefer something more versatile than the long white lace gown with the train and veil. Of course, if you are the lucky recipient of an heirloom dress—your grandmother's vintage white organdy or your aunt's Art Deco satin classic—thank your good fortune and wear it. But if not, there are many possibilities of attractive long dresses. You need not even choose white, although white, cream, or a very pale pastel is still most common. You might also consider a street-length cocktail dress (not too revealing, of course), which can look lovely on a bride when worn with the proper accessories. Or you may want to wear a suit: white linen for summer, with a big soft hat, flowers pinned to the lapel, and lacy Victorian gloves, or creamy white wool for winter, with a smart felt hat and a white silky scarf at the throat. You no longer have to go completely formal to be a beautiful bride.

If the bride is not to be formally attired, the groom can ease up a bit as well. Depending on the season, he may select a two- or three-piece suit in white, black, or navy, with a crisp shirt and a silk tie. He may also want to think about elegant accessories such as a silk handerkerchief in his breast pocket, good cuff links, and a flower in his buttonhole.

Part of the decision will rest upon the time of day the wedding is to be held. An evening wedding is usually more dressy than one held during the day. Make sure that your guests are aware of what is expected in their dress. They will feel most comfortable if they know in advance what to wear.

The dress worn by the wedding entourage is another consideration. Some couples prefer to have all the bridesmaids in identical dresses and the ushers in the same type of suit or tux. Others are more casual and simply choose a color and type of dress: all the girls in street-length peach or floor-length sky blue. The bride's dress generally dictates what the other members of the wedding party wear. If her dress is floor length, the bridesmaids should follow suit and the groom and ushers should wear tuxedos. If she is wearing a shorter dress, the bridesmaids again should take their cue from her.

A bridesmaid is usually expected to buy her own dress. That can be a costly proposition, especially after she has bought an engagement gift and a wedding gift as well. A thoughtful bride will not select the most expensive dress in the store; or, if she does and one of her bridesmaids has trouble with the price, she might offer to help with its purchase. She might also consider selecting a pattern that all the girls and their Moms can make. Why not organize a sewing bee for the wedding? You'll all save money, and have lots of fun too!

It is traditional for the bride to give the bridesmaids a small gift. It need not be expensive, but it should be appropriate—a small piece of jewelry, an article of clothing—to serve as a memento of a happy occasion shared.

The Wedding Party

The size of the wedding party generally has some relationship to the number of guests who attend the wedding ceremony. At larger functions, the bride may have a maid or matron of honor as well as several bridesmaids, who are in turn accompanied by their own ushers. There may also be a flower girl and a ring bearer. The best man, the male counterpart of the maid or matron of honor, is usually of the groom's choosing, although the ushers are selected jointly by the couple.

The maid of honor is usually the sister, cousin, or closest friend of the bride, and the bridesmaid's party is made up of her other near and dear friends and relatives. The ushers may be the boyfriends or fiancés of the bridesmaids, particularly if they are also friends of the bride and groom. If the couple prefer, however, they may select their own ushers.

The flower girl and ring bearer are usually the youngest members of the wedding party, and the younger siblings or cousins of the wedding pair are often asked to take those roles.

At small functions, the wedding party may consist solely of the maid of honor and the best man.

Often, the bride wants someone to give her away. Usually this role is performed by her father, who accompanies her down the aisle. If her father is not living, or not present for some other reason, it is appropriate to ask an older brother, cousin, or uncle to perform this service. A godfather or close family friend may also be asked to step in.

The Wedding Rehearsal

If you are having a sizable wedding party with a number of participants, you may want to have a brief rehearsal. Held just before the big event, it gives everyone a chance to move through their paces swiftly and easily and to get acquainted with their part. A wedding rehearsal is a good antidote for the pre-wedding jitters and reassures you that on the great day all will go well.

What's in a Name?

Once upon a time, every girl who had a ring slipped on her finger gave up her maiden name and became known to the world as "Mrs. John Doe" for the rest of her married life. Today modern and liberated young women are not so ready to give up their name, a precious evidence of identity that they have lived with all their lives.

If you want to follow tradition and change your name when you marry, it is your legal right, and many, many women still exercise it. But if you are of a different mind and want to keep your own name, you are also within your rights and should seek legal advice about how to do it.

Another alternative is use of the hyphenated name, such as

Carol Smith-Taber or Linda Wilkens-Gates. The first name in the combined name is the wife's; the second, her husband's. A question sometimes arises as to what the children are to be called if the wife maintains her name; the combined name can serve as the answer for that problem.

Photographs and the Wedding Album

Weddings are significant events both in the personal and the social sense. You should consider having yours photographed so that you preserve intact the memories of the joyful day. If you are concerned about the cost, you might think of asking a friend or relative handy with a camera to help out. You should, of course, expect to pay for the materials used, such as film, lights, and flashbulbs, as well as the cost of developing the film and making prints. When you are on a budget, remember that black-and-white film and processing costs are significantly cheaper than those for color. Pictures taken by an amateur photographer can have a particular charm of their own and can often capture a more intimate side of the event.

Professional photographers have their own approach to photographing a wedding. Some prefer formal posed shots, while others attempt to capture a more informal quality. You can decide which style suits you, and your wedding, the best. You can also ask to see samples of any professional's work; perhaps other wedding albums that he or she has done will give you some ideas about how to structure your own.

It is also nice to have pictures taken at various stages during the wedding, to get a sense of an event in progress. The photographer can snap the last-minute preparations of the bride as she adjusts her veil or sniffs her bouquet, the groom walking down the aisle, the shy smile of the little flower girl, the bridal couple's first dance as man and wife, and the parents of the bride at the end of the evening. Your finished album will tell you a wonderful story in pictures that you and your beloved will cherish forever.

The Big Day. . . . (For Her)

Well, this is IT! For many young women, their wedding day is one of the most important days of their life and they want to savor every minute of it. You should make sure that your big day is special too and indulge yourself in all kinds of luxurious treats throughout the day. If you can, do all of your errands and chores in advance, so that on the actual day you can have plenty of free time in which to pamper yourself.

Read the suggestions below, and see which ones appeal to you. Treat yourself to as many as you like, or let them be an inspiration to get your own imagination working and thinking of more ideas.

Breakfast in bed. Yes, you deserve it, so why not? Begin your day with such taste-tempting delights as freshly squeezed orange juice, pecan pancakes dripping with butter and real maple syrup, cranberry-nut muffins, steaming hot popovers, omelettes filled with savory cheese and spices, oatmeal with sliced apples, raisins, and cinnamon . . . Getting hungry? Good. Fix yourself a special tray, tuck the morning paper under your arm, and curl up and relax.

Your Hair. It is risky to get a brand-new haircut on your wedding day, but you should think about professional attention for your hair. A new hairdo may not work out, and this is a day when you want to look and feel your very best, so skip the surprises. Instead, indulge in a professional wash, set or blow-dry. Consider a good conditioning treatment, or a colorless henna rinse to bring your own natural highlights out of hiding. Your hair will sparkle and shine—and so will you!

Nails. Give yourself the treat of a professional manicure and pedicure. Choose a pretty pastel shade that will go well with (but not overpower) your dress: pink, peach, coral, or rose are good choices; avoid bright red, scarlet, cherry, and wine. Sit back and let your nails be soaked, snipped, buffed, and polished into perfect trimmed elegance.

Skin and cosmetics. Having a facial is another wonderful

wedding-day treat. What a great way to get your complexion rosy and glowing! A professional skin care specialist will analyze your skin type and give you the proper treatment for skin that is oily, dry, or delicate. Each type has its own special requirements; let a pro tell you how to do it. Many salons will also do your makeup. Remember, less *is* more; you don't need bright red lips, vampy eyes, deeply rouged cheeks. Let your own natural good looks shine out: Nothing transforms a face like happiness.

Privacy. At some point during the day, you should retreat from everyone and spend some quiet time alone. This is a big day, and you may want a few moments to reflect on its meaning in private. Soak in a hot tub filled with bubbles or scented bath oil, write in a journal or diary, listen to your favorite piece of music, or just close your eyes and snooze for a little while. Your mind and body will feel rested and recharged.

The Honeymoon

Like all good things, even a wedding finally does come to an end. The two of you are no doubt thrilled and delighted to finally belong legally to each other, but you are also doubtless very tired, and maybe even a little let down. After all, your lives *do* have to resume their ordinary rhythms and routines, and that can feel just a little deflating after the hectic pace and excitement of your pre-wedding schedule.

That is precisely why the honeymoon is so important for newly married couples. It gives you a chance to get away and put a special, even magical little buffer between the wedding and everyday life. You need this time together to rediscover all the wonderful things about each other that made you fall in love and marry in the first place.

When planning your honeymoon, you realize that finances play a major role. Weddings are expensive, and you may not have the funds to take your dream vacation. But even if your money is limited, your imagination needn't be. Let your sense of adventure run wild. If it means camping in the Blue Ridge

Mountains or renting a beachside cottage off-season, you can still have a marvelous time.

Many couples plan for their honeymoon right along with the wedding and budget themselves accordingly. A resort honeymoon is very common; places often selected are the Virgin Islands, the Bahamas, Mexico, Florida, and California. If your funds won't permit that, however, why not spend one fabulous weekend at a four-star hotel? The stay will be short, but you may find it more enjoyable and restful than a week somewhere less elegant. Champagne breakfasts, dancing till dawn—it can be two days of sheer delight.

Thank-You Notes

Newly married couples may find themselves with literally dozens of gifts that have poured in from all over—distant relatives, long-lost friends, business associates of their parents—and little idea of how to handle this overwhelming display of generosity. Cards become detached from gifts, and it is easy to forget who sent what. Dealing with the situation gradually begins to seem insurmountable.

Don't fall into that trap. Keep a careful list of all the gifts as they arrive, with notations of the date of arrival, the name and address of the sender, and a brief description of the item. Many couples try to write their thank-you notes in alphabetical order, which is a mistake, since that is not the order in which they were received. What if your Abbott cousins send their present four weeks after your friend Brad Wyman? It is more important, then, to send the notes according to when you received the gift.

Keeping a succinct "gift journal" will help enormously, especially if you receive three blenders, two bathroom scales, and four tea sets. It's always nice to say something specific and personal about the gift that you are acknowledging.

The message should be hand-written, in ink. Many couples have note cards printed with their names engraved on the outside and a blank space for a message inside. A few lines will suffice: Address the giver by name, make reference to the gift, saying that it is useful/beautiful/unusual/thoughtful, and sign it with the appropriate closing.

If the task becomes tedious, break it up and write three to five notes a day. Check the names off your list to avoid confusion. And remember, it is thoughtful for both the bride and groom to sign the card.

When You're the Guest

A few helpful hints about wedding etiquette:

Do find out in advance what kind of attire is expected. You will feel out of place in a casual sport jacket if the rest of the men are in tuxedos or tails.

Don't try to upstage the bride. Girls, don't wear white if you know that she is, and your dress should not be too showy or attention-getting. This is her day to shine; wait your turn for your day in the sun.

Don't bring uninvited guests. Weddings are highly personal and meaningful events. The guests should be invited at the discretion of the bride and groom.

Do spend some time selecting a gift that is in keeping with your income, taste, and personal feelings about the couple. Make sure you include a card that identifies it.

Do congratulate the bride and groom personally at some point after the ceremony. Since it is usually the parents of one or both of the couple who are footing the bill, it is always nice to make a point of exchanging a few words with your hosts.

Unravelling the Mystery—What to Buy

Buying the right wedding gift can be difficult. You want something that is personal, useful, and distinctive and that won't cost a fortune. Below are some suggestions for choosing a gift that will be ideally suited to the occasion.

Be Traditional. Many brides still register in department and specialty stores. The bride may list her selection of china, silverware, crystal, cookware, and even a color scheme for sheets, towels, and other linens. Any of those categories provides ample room for generous and thoughtful gift-giving. Even a small item, such as a serving platter to match her dishes, or guest towels coordinated with her new bathroom, will be especially welcome because they're things she would have chosen for herself. Most stores also keep a record of what items have already been purchased, so you run less risk of duplicating a gift selection.

Be Creative. Think about giving a one-of-a-kind, unique, and special gift—one that you make yourself! Consider your own skills: Do you paint, draw, or photograph especially well? What about choosing one of your own creations (or creating one just for the occasion) and having it framed to be hung or displayed in the couple's new home? Do you sew or knit? How about stitching up a tablecloth and matching napkins, a set of patchwork pillows for the sofa, or matching ski sweater and mitten sets for the bride and groom?

Let your own imagination and talent lead the way to a completely innovative and original gift.

Be Helpful. After the wedding, you can usually predict that the bride and groom will be worn out from all the festivities. What about treating them to a special postwedding supper, a play, or a night on the town? Or you can offer to prepare a home-cooked meal, such as breakfast, served on some postwedding morning. Such treats can be greatly appreciated pick-me-ups after the excitement has died down.

LIVING TOGETHER

Times Are Changing

Once upon a time, two people who chose to live together without the formality of either a legal or religious ceremony faced losing the approbation of society.

They could, at the very least, count on facing the anger of parents and family, the scorn of neighbors, and the embarrassment, coldness, or confusion of friends. Living together outside of marriage was a pretty sure way to cut yourself off from a lot of people, very quickly.

Not so today. Many young couples (and some who are not so young) are electing to live together in a state that resembles marriage in all ways—except that they aren't married. People choose to do this for many reasons, and they are not considered immoral, indecent, or in any way objectionable by most people, including their families.

The decision to enter into a relationship of this kind is as serious and personal as marriage; no one can make up your mind about such an issue for you. Some young people are wholly comfortable with the idea and can easily see themselves in such a situation. Others feel that it is not for them now, nor will it ever be. Whatever your feelings, however, you will probably encounter the situation more and more as you grow older, and you should know how to deal with it appropriately.

Deciding to Do It

Keep in mind that living together is a serious commitment and should not be undertaken lightly, no matter how public opinion seems to view it. Although you will not have the legal entanglements created by marriage, you do develop very strong attachments to a live-in boyfriend or girlfriend. Breaking up can be traumatic, whether you have the ring and the piece of paper or not.

Think carefully about whether or not you are ready to commit yourself in this way. You need to weigh the pros and cons before you decide. Talk it over thoroughly with your prospective "roommate" before you go ahead, in the hope of avoiding serious misunderstandings later.

Telling the Folks

No matter how liberal society at large may be, parents tend to react a little more strongly on this particular issue. It is best to tell them openly and honestly, and as soon as you feel you can. Don't avoid answering phones, or start making excuses about why they never seem to find you in your dorm room anymore. Your new relationship doesn't need the additional strain of hostile parents, so tell them early to avoid resentment building up.

Avoiding Embarrassment

When you have friends who are living together but not married, how do you treat them? As a married couple? Or just as boyfriend and girlfriend? Are there any rules left to follow?

You should take your cue from them and the signals they are sending out. In most cases living together is pretty serious business, and that commitment should be reflected in your social responses. On the other hand, however, don't assume that the couple will marry eventually. Some couples use this as a trial period to see how they like domestic life; others have serious moral or philosophical objections to being married and have no intention of ever legally "tying the knot."

At dinners, parties, and other social functions, both partners should be invited. You may also wish to seat them together if other couples are being seated similarly. If you have had a special friendship with one member of the pair, feel free to pursue it independently of the "couple" relationship; you need not invite Jim along every time you meet Jane for a movie and a slice of pizza But in planning large, important or formal occasions, inviting both is the proper thing to do.

You may wonder how to introduce a couple who are living together but unmarried. Or as part of such a couple you may find yourself with an awkward case of the stutters as you say, "I'd like you to meet Jason, my, um, um, um . . ."

It is true that there is no word yet that adequately describes this nonformalized union of adults. "Friend" seems coy; "spouse" is dishonest; "boyfriend" or "girlfriend" leaves something out; and "lover" is too specific. In the face of all that, what *can* you say?

In a pinch, "friend" will suffice, as will "boyfriend" or "girl-friend." Avoid the outright lie of "husband" or "wife" and the illicit overtones of "lover." You can always circumvent the problem by dropping the title altogether and simply saying, "I'd like you to meet Karen, Bob, Bill . . ." or whomever and leave it at that.

Basically, living with someone else in this way still takes the courage of one's convictions, despite the prevalent permissive attitudes. If you are going to do it at all, it should be done with openness, directness, and pride.

CHAPTER X

Say It Right!

The way you speak—your voice, your tone, your syntax and grammar—lets people know a great deal about the kind of person you are. Why not make that impression a positive one by learning to speak in the most articulate and effective way possible?

As a budding adult, you need to learn to speak effectively so that you can function optimally at school, socially, and eventually in the workplace.

Being aware of what you're saying and how you're saying it is the first step; then you can begin to develop the kinds of habits that will hold up for a lifetime.

Talking to Adults

If you've studied a romance language such as French or Spanish, you know that such languages have two distinct forms of address: the formal and the familiar. Although English no longer preserves this distinction, there are still formal and less formal ways of address; when talking to adults, you should generally opt for the more formal of the two.

That means, for instance, that unless you are specifically invited to do otherwise, you should address your teachers, the parents of your friends, and the friends of your parents as Mr., Mrs., and Miss. Even within your own family, it may be considered disrespectful to address certain older relatives without using "Aunt" or "Uncle" before the name.

Some topics of conversation are considered impolite to introduce, especially with an elder. These topics include any kind of intimate talk about sex, money, religion, or politics. Keep in mind that should someone, even an older person, begin such a conversation with you, you are free to decline participation in it. Either politely change the subject or simply say in a nice tone of voice, "If you don't mind, I'd rather not discuss that."

You and Your Friends

You don't have to worry about friends, you think; you can say anything to a friend, right? Wrong! It is precisely because we love and respect our friends that we want to be careful and thoughtful about what we say to them.

Remember that a good friend:

- respects confidences by waiting for them to be offered, listening to them respectfully when they are, and never repeating them to anyone else...
- is free with compliments...
- offers criticism kindly, and not without saying something positive...
- avoids wounding personal remarks such as, "Gained some weight, haven't you?" or "Gee, that's not a very flattering dress/haircut/pair of pants/etc., is it?"

The Social Circuit

Dress-up parties, dances, informal get-togethers: your social life is filled with all kinds of exciting activities. What do you say at a social function that gets you noticed in the right way? Here are a few tips:

- Do remember to mingle with a number of people at an event. Even if you just exchange a few words, it is considered more gracious behavior than spending an entire evening talking to one or two friends.
- Do remember to ask questions and listen for the answers; a good conversation is a dialogue, not a monologue.

- Don't gossip, especially about another guest, or even worse, the host or hostess; you could easily be overheard.

CONVERSATION STARTERS AND STOPPERS

A brilliant raconteur can regale the company on almost any subject, but most of us are not so gifted. You should therefore keep in mind that some topics of conversation will stimulate and delight your listeners, whereas others will go over like the proverbial lead balloon. Which to seek and which to shun? Read on!

Good to Shout About in a Crowd

- Any new and exciting movie/play/concert/art exhibit you have recently seen or attended.
- A fantastic new book: mystery, romance, biography, thriller.
- A trip you've taken or are planning to take, especially if your destination is foreign or in any way unusual.
- School: New teachers, classes, extracurricular activities; college plans. Don't however, give detailed information about grades—yours or anyone else's; it's considered bad manners.
- Summer vacation: Plans for an exciting or different one; exotic travel, unusual job.
- Current events: Great if you're up for an argument. People can get deeply involved with political issues, so be sure you're ready to support what you say with facts and to back it up with fervor!

To Avoid Like the Plague

- Sex: It will get you noticed all right, but definitely in the wrong way.
- Other people: As suggested above, public gossip makes you sound mean-spirited and petty.
- The weather: An old standby, but try to do better.

- Illness: Yes, it's a fact of life, but why add gloom to the discussion by bringing it up?

YOU AND YOUR VOCABULARY

You may think that your present vocabulary is perfectly adequate to express your thoughts and ideas, and you are probably right. But the English language, with its remarkable abundance of expressive words, is something that you should utilize to the fullest in your daily speech. For that reason, you should try to improve your vocabulary and thereby expand your oral abilities. The actual thoughts you have to express are profoundly affected by the words you have with which to say them.

Increasing your verbal capacity needn't be difficult; think of it as a kind of mental challenge or game. Always look up a new and unfamiliar word that you encounter in reading or in conversation. Make an effort to use that new word soon, so that it really becomes your own. Be sure to note the correct pronunciation and usage, though: nothing sounds sillier or more pretentious than misuse of a big, important-sounding word. If you're not certain about the meaning or usage, consult your English teacher or the school librarian.

Enlist the help of your friends in learning new words too; try to stump one another with words you've found. Flipping through the dictionary for unusual or interesting words can be fun. Nor should you overlook the help offered by amusements such as Scrabble and crossword puzzles. You can find lots of entertaining possibilities for making your word power grow.

Just for fun, see how many of these words you know without looking them up. Can you use each correctly in a sentence? Look up any words you don't know or fully understand the proper usage of. Just think: Your vocabulary is growing already...

aegis	firmament
agape	gauche
allege	hovel

bilateral	irreparable
bucolic	jocose
compendium	monolithic
contentious	palindrome
deplorable	remunerate
elucidate	vestigial
enclave	veneer
endorse	venal
fiat	warble
flotsam	weir
furrow	zenith

Having a vivid and varied vocabulary is a nice way to make sure that what you say is heard—and remembered.

CORRECT GRAMMAR

While this book is not intended as a comprehensive grammatical text, it is worth noting some common spoken errors so that you can start correcting them now.

Real vs. Really

We commonly hear remarks such as "It was a real good book" or "I had a real nice time," but neither one is correct. "Real" is an adjective that refers to something that is true, in the way that a fact is "real." It can also mean "genuine" or "complete." "Really" is an adverb that means "in fact," "positively," or "indeed." Correct usage demands the phrase "really happy" or "really pretty."

Lay vs. Lie

These two words are often confused but in fact don't mean the same thing at all. "Lay" means to place or put, as in "Lay your cards on the table"; "lie" means "to rest," "to recline." Some of the confusion arises from the fact that the past tense of "lie" is also "lay," so that you would say, "Yesterday, I lay down for a nap..." The verb "lay," however, has "laid" as its past tense. If you keep the meaning in mind when you speak, you ought to be able to use the two correctly.

Disinterested/Uninterested

"Disinterested" means "unbiased or impartial, with no thought of personal gain or advantage," whereas "uninterested" means "lacking interest or indifferent." Thus, you can be interested in a subject or argument about which you are also disinterested.

Double Prepositions

When two words that can function as prepositions appear together, one is often superfluous. Thus, "outside" usually means the same as "outside of." "From among," "inside of," "of from," and "off of" are other double prepositions that should be avoided.

Other grammatical mistakes are far too numerous and complicated to explain here. Suffice it to say that grammar is a subject to which you should pay close attention in school. All too many teens think that grammar is boring and unimportant, and they come away from school not knowing the basics of oral communication. But people judge you on the basis of what you say and how you say it, so don't make this mistake. If you learn grammar now, it will effortlessly become a part of your natural speech pattern.

A Case Against Slang

Certain kinds of slang expressions, such as "ain't" for "aren't"; "dunno" for "don't know"; "gonna" for "going to," and "ya" for "you" (to name just a few), have become in-creasingly popular, not only in spoken usage, but in print as well. And yet for all their popularity, such expressions are not proper usage and should be avoided. Although you may feel they are appropriate in casual conversation, verbal habits are quick to be formed and hard to break, and you may find yourself using a slang expression when you neither want nor intend to do so. You should therefore prevent these habits from forming at all and try to speak correctly in all situations, formal and informal alike.

An even stronger case can be made against the use of certain four-letter words. Not only are they offensive and vulgar, but their use will quickly brand you as someone lacking imagination and originality in speech—do you really want to create an impression like that? Although the use of such language may impress some of your peers, it won't help you develop the kind of vocabulary that is the hallmark of real sophistication and intelligence. Reach for real, carefully considered words each time you speak, and you'll develop an eloquence that will last a lifetime.

TALKING ON THE TELEPHONE

When you speak on the telephone, you can't modify your words with a gesture or facial expression. Your voice and your words are the only things that your listener has, so you should try to make them say exactly what you mean.

When You're the Caller

When calling the home of a friend or schoolmate, it's best to identify yourself first and then politely ask if you may speak to Billy, Karen, or Bob. When your friend picks up, you may want to identify yourself again, in case the in-formation was not relayed. If your friend isn't at home, ask to leave a message, or try to establish a time to call back. Be sure to ask how late (or early) in the day you may conveniently call. If you're calling a teacher, an older friend/relative, or anyone related to business (someone whose car you wash, children you tend, etc.), ask for the person first, using Mr., Mrs., or Miss. Then identify yourself. And remember to speak clearly and audibly at all times: No mumbling!

Answering the Phone

Remember that if you're waiting for a call, picking up on the first ring may make you seem too eager, especially in a social context. It is considered appropriate to pick up on the third ring in most personal or social situations. Note, however, that in a business context, picking up sooner is considered better.

If you take messages for your parents, siblings, or in any business situation, be sure to get the correct message, spelling of the caller's name, and number where he or she can be reached. Don't assume that the area code will be the same as the one you're in. Be sure to relay all messages promptly. If you receive a phone message yourself, it's considered proper—especially in a business matter—to return the call within two or three hours. Finally, whether you're the caller or the called, be sure that your voice on the phone is friendly, light, and open.

Dialing a Date

If you are calling to ask a girl (or, in these liberated times, a guy) for a date, you're bound to be nervous. What can you say to ease your anxiety and help get the answer you want to hear? Well, there's no sure-fire method, but some ways of asking do work better than others.

For example, you should not begin by saying: "Hello, Lisa? This is Kirk. I was wondering if you're busy on Saturday night...?" If you ask that way, Lisa won't know what you're asking her for; maybe you want her to help you clean the family rec room! Moreover, she may really want to see you, but only on condition that you aren't inviting her to a movie that she has no interest in seeing or a party at the house of someone she doesn't like. Better (and more gracious) to phrase your question like this: "Hello, Lisa? This is Kirk. I was calling to ask if you might want to attend the Friday night dance at the gym with me. I could pick you up around eight." This lets her know what the invitation is for, not just who is making it. And it leaves her free to say, "Kirk, I'd love to go to the dance, but I have to baby-sit for my little sister that night. Maybe you could stop by for a while to visit...?" So remember, guys and gals, when you're making dates, be as clear and specific about the invitation as you can. After all, a clear, friendly invitation says a lot about the person making it, and that something is quite positive indeed.

Your Voice

Haven't you noticed that the meaning of words is frequently affected by the tone of voice in which they are uttered? If someone at home were to snarl, "Are you going to clean up your room, young lady?" you would probably feel guilty, hurt, and angry. And you certainly wouldn't be in any hurry to clean up your room! But if that same question were said in a gentle and cheerful way, you would probably feel much better about doing the chore.

Keeping that in mind, you can use your voice—its pitch, intensity, and volume—to help get your message across. Do you want to offer sympathy or comfort? Then keep your voice low and soft. Trying to cheer up a friend? Use a more enthusiastic, positive tone. Want to get your sister or brother to help with a household chore? Then avoid a tone dripping with sarcasm, or laced with frustration and annoyance.

THE UNSPOKEN MESSAGE

Along with your voice, your gestures are an important conveyor of meaning. Many times, a person's unspoken language—made up of hands, eyes, body—will give signals about the message behind the words. For that reason, you should always be conscious of what your nonverbal language is telling your listener.

Your Eyes

Do make frequent eye contact with your listener. Failure to look someone in the eyes makes it seem as if you have something to hide or are not telling the truth. Don't stare, but don't be afraid to look, openly and candidly, at the person to whom you are speaking.

Your Hands

Don't fiddle with things—pen, pencil, soda can, straw—while you're talking to someone; it will distract them from what you are saying. Keep your hands unobtrusively at your sides if you're standing or in your lap if you're sitting. Really to shun: nail-biting, twirling a lock of hair, fingers in mouth or on face.

Body Talk

The same rules apply. Avoid fidgeting—shifting from one leg to the other, tapping with your foot, crossing and uncrossing your legs. Don't feel you have to be a statue, but if you can't sit relatively still during a conversation, you'll make your listener wonder why you're so jumpy.

You Said a Mouthful

Besides the actual words it utters, your mouth says a lot.

Keep your expression pleasant, and smile frequently. Not a big and obviously insincere grin, but a friendly, I-just-thought-of-something-nice sort of smile. Watch how it does wonders to put your listener at ease. Needless to say, a constant frown or pout will get you labeled a sourpuss, so why not dazzle 'em with those pearly whites instead?

PUBLIC SPEAKING

Speaking before a large group can be unnerving, especially if you haven't had much experience at doing it. But learning to handle yourself in a poised and graceful manner before a crowd is one of the hallmarks of adulthood. No set of rules can eliminate anxiety completely, but remembering a few basic points may help to keep it in check.

First, at what sort of event or occasion will you be speaking? School rally? Community or church event? Social gathering? Knowing the setting will help determine not only what you're going to say, but how you're going to say it. Do you want to make a serious and formal impression? Delight them with your wit and charm? Rouse their emotions about an important issue or cause? You need to settle upon a persona for your speech so that you can decide how best to achieve the impression you want.

Next, will you be reading from a prepared text or speaking spontaneously? Keep in mind that straight reading from a text can be a bit dull for your listeners. Instead, many professional speakers elect to speak from notes; they don't read, but they do have something to which they can refer. And if it's okay for professionals, why not for you? Remember too that whether you're reading from a prepared text or speaking from notes, it's important to make eye contact with your audience at regular intervals. Look up at one person's face for a moment, holding your gaze steady. Make sure that you select a different face from time to time, too; you don't want to stare at anyone. But focusing on one person will keep your eyes from wandering restlessly (read: nervously) all over the room.

Also important is the delivery of your words. Practice projecting your voice from your chest without shouting; really make your voice carry. Be sure to enunciate clearly, with full, round vowels and distinct consonants. You might even want to practice with a tape recorder before an important speech such as a campaign speech for the school election or a class presentation you are giving. That way, you can listen objectively for rough spots and smooth them out beforehand.

If you are going to be speaking for any length of time, don't forget to have a small glass of water nearby; you can sip it to revive a tired, dry throat.

If you have a part in a church or school play, naturally you won't have notes (unless cue cards are provided!), but some of the other tips given here might come in handy. When you speak to another character in the play, of course you will give him or her your undivided attention. But during an extended speech or soliloquy, be sure to make eye contact now and then—remember, here's where you really do want to communicate with your audience. Take deep, slow breaths if you're nervous; it's important to slow down your heart rate, and get your breathing back to normal. Always pronounce your lines clearly and distinctly and project your voice to the very last rows of the house. That final, hearty applause will let know that your efforts have not been wasted.

The Last Word...

A few final tips on how to say it right, every time:

- In response to a question that you haven't heard or clearly understood, say, "I beg your pardon?" or "Excuse me?" or even "Could you please repeat that?" Never, under any circumstances, say "Huh?" or

"What?" Both of those responses are extremely rude and should be eliminated from your speech entirely.

- Talking and eating don't mix! When you have something in your mouth, keep mum until you've finished it.
- Avoid "newspeak" at all costs! Although technology may have taken over all other aspects of our lives, it should not take over our language. Never say, "It impacted on," but instead, "It had an impact upon." Remember that "guesstimate" is not a word, no matter what anybody tells you! Don't use such "automatic" language, even if it has become all too common; instead, make an effort to speak precisely and beautifully, using your own means of expression.
- Finally, remember that "please," "thank you," and "I'm sorry" are some of the most important words in the English language, so don't stint—use them often and with sincerity.

Index

134

friends of, 4
respect for, 2–3, 7
telling, of engagement, 98
party
college, 82
dressing for, 38
engagement, 101
throwing, 21, 24–27
plans
confirming date, 45
sharing with parents, 5
travel, 84–85
posture, 29
precautions, in foreign travel, 93–94
privacy
emotional, 7
need for, 5, 6
respecting roommate's, 72, 89
in stepfamily, 11
professors, 79–80
proposal of marriage, 96–98
public speaking, 131–132
punctuality, 2, 16, 45, 59, 61

R
reception, wedding, 106–107
rehearsal, wedding, 111
relationship
friendly, 15
meaningful, 13
with roommate, 73–74
respect
atmosphere of, 7
for confidences, 122
for family members, 1, 2
for friends, 14, 17
for home, 18
for older family members, 11
for parents, 2–3, 4
for siblings, 5
responsibility
in blended family, 11
for car use, 9–10
in college life, 75
for elderly, 12
for home relationship, 4
as host-hostess, 24
in romance, 50
résumé, preparing, 58
romance
break-up of, 55–56
first, 50–51
with professor, 80
telling parents of, 98
room
bridal shower, 100
college, 74–75
hotel, 89
roommate, dormitory, 72–74

rules
for being a guest, 18–20
for dorm living, 72–73
for first date, 44–46
in group travel, 90–91
for having guests, 18
obeying, 2–3
on-the-job, 61–62
social, 15–16, 77, 81
for speaking, 131–133

S
school
dressing for, 30, 37–38
finding dates at, 42
making friends at, 13
schoolwork, 2
helping others with, 72
scheduling, 79
self-assurance, 43–44
sex, teenage, 51–53, 81
shower, wedding, 99–100
siblings, 5–6
respect for, 7
step-, 10–11
skills, advertising your, 57–58
slang, 126–127
stag party, 100–101
stationery, 65, 67
stepparents, 10–11
study, college, 77–79, 82
style, personal, 30–31

T
telephone, 1, 8
before visiting, 17
limiting calls, 8, 72
listening in, 7
long-distance, 95
private, 8
talking on, 127–129
thank-you note, 68, 102, 105, 115–116
topics, letter-writing, 65–66
train travel, 85
travel, 84–95
typewriter, 67

V
vocabulary, improving, 124–125
voice, 127, 129

W
wedding
album, 112
party, 110–111
planning, 102–103
weekend visit
to college, 70–71
dress for, 30
tips for, 20
travel on, 84
words, new, 124–125
writing, 64–69